IDEAS
THAT
STICK!

See idea **217:** "an unforgettable birthday" ➡

Artwork by Stephanie Bagayawa

Post-it® Brand

IDEAS THAT STICK!

222 Ingenious, Creative, Practical, and Simply Preposterous Ways of Using Post-it® Notes

A Fireside Book
Published by Simon & Schuster
New York London Toronto Sydney

FIRESIDE
Rockefeller Center
1230 Avenue of the Americas
New York, NY 10020

For information regarding special discounts for bulk purchases, please contact Simon & Schuster Special Sales at (800) 456-6798 or business@simonandschuster.com.

Set in Berthold Akzidenz Grotesk, Felt Tip, Helvetica Neue, and ITC Franklin Gothic.

Manufactured in Singapore by
Tien Wah Press (Pte.) Ltd.

10 9 8 7 6 5 4 3 2 1

Library of Congress Catalog Card Number:
2005051379

ISBN-13: 978- 0-7432-8431-8
ISBN-10:   0-7432-8431-3

Post-It®
Ideas That Stick!
was conceived and produced
by Weldon Owen Inc.
814 Montgomery Street
San Francisco, CA 94133

WELDON OWEN INC.
Chief Executive Officer John Owen
President & Chief Operating Officer Terry Newell
Chief Financial Officer Christine E. Munson
Vice President, Publisher Roger Shaw
Vice President, International Sales Stuart Laurence
Creative Director Gaye Allen
Production Director Chris Hemesath
Color Manager Teri Bell

Series Manager Brynn Breuner
Art Director Colin Wheatland
Senior Designer Lisa Milestone
Designer Alec Nikolajevich
Art Assistance Renée Meyers
Contributing Editors Jennifer Block Martin,
Elizabeth Dougherty, Galen Gruman,
Norman Kolpas, Debbie MacKinnon
Editorial Assistant Lucie Parker
Proofreaders Desne Ahlers,
Gail Nelson-Bonebrake, David Sweet
Indexer Ken DellaPenta

A Weldon Owen Production

Artwork by Crystal Rae

contents

motivating

how about those sales reports?

raising a family

Artwork by Tamara-Rose Croxall

foreword

Life without Post-it® Notes? It's hard to imagine. In 1974, frustrated by bookmarks that kept falling out of his hymnal, 3M researcher Art Fry tinkered with a sticky coating that his colleague Spencer Silver had invented six years earlier. The result? The incredible, indispensable Post-it® Note. How far those little canary-yellow notes have come since their debut in 1980! No longer confined to the office, Post-it® Notes have become a global icon and a universal tool for fast and effective communication. These bold visual cues have revolutionized our lives, helping us manage, organize, and, of course, remember. The newest member of the Post-it® product family is the Post-it® Super Sticky Note, designed to hold that thought even stronger and longer to vertical surfaces. As you'll see from the following real life tips and tricks for the note that sticks, Post-it® Notes have inspired people worldwide to find better ways to brainstorm, plan, play, create, and much more. Unleash your imagination—and see what this sticky superstar can do for you!

See idea 23: "ahh, yes, a little to the left…" ➡

learning

"Tell me and I'll forget. Show me and I may remember," goes an old Chinese proverb, "but involve me and I'll understand." Whether you're trying to make homework more fun or simply learning a few words in a language in preparation for your travels, the more you make learning a hands-on experience, the easier it is to retain information. Or, to put it another way, we learn by doing.

helping your children learn

For kids, learning is all about making connections between ideas or concepts and their real-world counterparts. Find ways to help your kids turn learning into play and they'll be more likely to make learning a lifelong passion.

1

letter by letter

When my preschooler started learning the alphabet, I made her a set of capital and lowercase letters, writing each pair of letters on an individual Post-it® Note. When we went out in the car, she'd bring those notes with her and stick them to the back of the seat in front of her whenever she recognized a letter on a sign or billboard. It helped her connect letters in books to the real world around her.

Steve S., Ardmore, PA

2

i can do it by myself

After my four-year-old son recognized all the letters, he was ready to learn more. So I used Post-it® Notes to label the drawers, cupboards, and toy bins in his room with bold words and simple drawings. He's delighted with the increased autonomy that comes with knowing the names of his things and his "big boy" ability to put them away where they belong. Best of all, he's beginning to recognize whole words and is eager to spell everything.

Emma F., London, England

3

dressing yourself

We used Post-it® Notes when my daughter was learning to dress herself. I would draw a picture of each piece of clothing—boots, jumper, trousers, socks, and so on—on a note and then pass each note to her. She loved to stick each one where it belonged.

Gillian M., Halifax, England

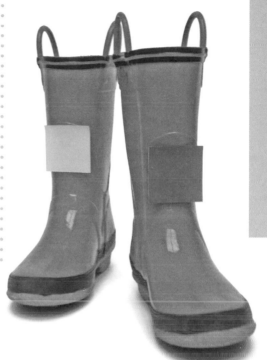

4

left or right?

My young son had a tough time telling left from right. To give him visual cues, I stuck blue Post-it® Notes on his left sleeves, pant legs, boots, mittens, and shoes, and yellow ones on all the rights. The deal we made was that when he correctly identified the left or right side of a piece of clothing, he got to pull off the note and add it to a pile. After collecting 20 notes, he could trade them in for a treat—perhaps a trip to the zoo or a new book. Now, he's got his lefts and rights down better than I do!

Anna D., Des Moines, IA

5

signs of success

When my daughter was learning to read, she started sounding out simple words like "sugar" that she saw around the house. I encouraged her efforts by using Post-it® Notes in a fun way. I would write a word on a note, then stick the note where she could find the items. "Sugar" went inside the baking cupboard, "beans" by the canned goods, and so on. Today, we play a drive-by version of this game in the car: when she sees a word like "parking" or "stop" on a sign, she sticks her note with the corresponding word on her window.

Gillian M., Halifax, England

6

expanding vocabulary

I'm a teacher and use Post-it® Notes to help my students increase their vocabulary with this simple exercise: I write a word on a note and stick it on the chalkboard. The children are asked to write out synonyms for that word on more notes, then they stick them underneath the first note. They keep adding notes until all the synonyms they know are up on the board.

Isabelle G., Tallahassee, FL

7

tackling new words

In our school, we use Post-it® Notes to cover up certain words in board books. This alerts our young readers that they are about to read a word that is unfamiliar, so they know they need to get their mouths ready to sound out the first syllable. They love to peel off a note to reveal the "secret word."

Jennifer M., Fresno, CA

8

practicing times tables

My seven-year-old practices her multiplication tables with Post-it® Notes. I write "1 x" on a note, continuing with "2 x," "3 x," and so on, up to 12. I repeat this process with another 12 notes, this time pairing the numbers with an equal sign. We stick the notes to the table in pairs (for example, "2 x 6 =") and put a blank note next to them. My daughter writes the answer on the blank.

Laura B., Auckland, New Zealand

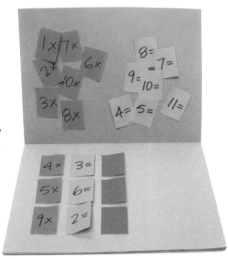

9

improving spelling skills

When my child brings home spelling words from school, we practice with Post-it® Notes. He copies each word onto a note, and we cover that note with a blank one. When I call out the word, he writes it down on the top note. If he gets stuck, he simply lifts the top note to check the correct spelling on the note underneath.

Diego R., Bilbao, Spain

10

geek-free address book

On a recent flight, I noticed that the passenger sitting next to me had a stack of well-used, small Post-it® Notes stuck to the back of his cell phone. Curious, I asked him what they were for. He replied that he was a kindergarten teacher and couldn't be bothered to enter in all the names and numbers of his students every year, and found it easier just to use the pad of notes. (He also admitted that he had no idea how to use the address book function on his phone—and no interest in learning!)

Marie P., Bognoli, Italy

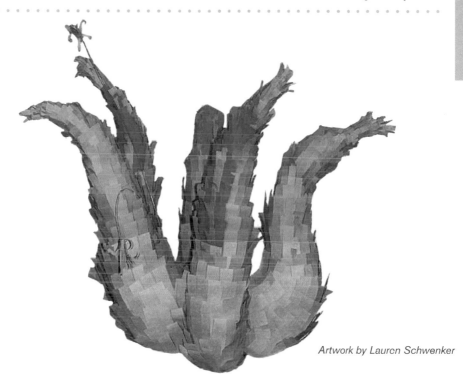

Artwork by Lauren Schwenker

11

flag songs for recitals

We use Post-it® Notes to identify the songs our kids need to play during piano recitals and to number them in the correct order. They can then quickly flip to the correct page in the songbook and not have to search during their performance. It's one more source of anxiety I can help remove.

Julie H., Oakland, CA

12

advice from the teacher

Our daughter's cello teacher is passionate about Post-it® Notes. At every lesson, he sticks little reminders next to individual bars or phrases in her piece with advice such as "Count the beats" or "Stretch your fourth finger higher." The presence of these notes makes our daughter feel like the teacher is right there with her when she practices at home.

Peyton B., Paris, France

When you see an F#, use your third finger!

13 piano navigation

To make it easier for my beginning pianist to get oriented, I wrote the names of the piano keys on small Post-it® Notes and stuck them on or just above each key for the middle octave. Then I added notes for all of the C's so she could see the key pattern. As it got easier for her to know where to start playing, I took the notes away—leaving just middle C.

Roger S., London, England

adult learning

Who said old dogs can't learn new tricks? Learning is easy for a grown-up of any age if you break up subjects into bite-sized pieces of easy-to-digest information. Approach a subject in this way and you'll feel like the world has become your feast of knowledge.

14

learning a language

I'm studying French. To help me improve my vocabulary, I place Post-it® Notes on objects all around my house with their names written in French on the front (and in English on the back so I can make sure that I'm right). For example, I stuck a note labeled "la porte" on my front door.

Lauren L., Crownsville, MD

le tableau

la lampe

le bureau

la plante

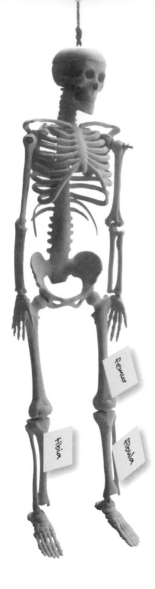

15

bone by bone

The first year of medical school feels like a constant exercise in memorizing every single part of the human body. For some reason, I had a particular block about learning bone names (there are 206 bones in an adult!)—until I tried Post-it® Notes. I used the notes as small flags to label, in tiny printing, every piece on a full-size resin study skeleton. Then I'd step back far enough so I couldn't read the names. As soon as I could positively identify a bone, I'd remove its flag and stick it randomly to the wall; then I'd step up and study those bones whose labels remained. When all the notes were on the wall, I'd do the exercise in reverse, returning the labels to the bones.

Ariel S., Detroit, MI

Artwork by Richard Sears

16

foldable squadron

During a summer internship at an engineering company, I was given a large stack of three-inch-square Post-it® Notes. I needed to find something to do with them, so I decided to design a small paper airplane that actually flew, with as high an aspect ratio as possible, almost a flying wing. By the end of the summer, I had created a whole air force of gliders (made during lunch breaks, of course). Here are instructions on how you can make one of my favorites yourself.

Jeff L., Wichita Falls, TX

To make your own flying wing from a
Post-it® Note, follow these steps:

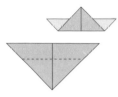

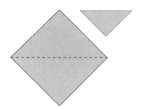

1 Fold a note in half
diagonally, with the sticky
part on the outside and
the tip pointed down.

2 Crease the resulting
triangle over its midline,
bending the flaps toward you,
but do not leave it folded.

3 Fold the tip of the triangle
up over itself; the fold should
be a third of the way from the
top, as shown above.

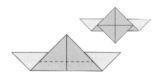

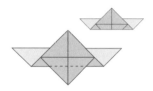

4 Unfold the front flap of the
triangle at the midline to create
a diamond extending below the
wing, as shown above.

5 Fold the part of the
diamond that falls below the
base back behind the base,
tucking it under and behind

6 Fold the bottom edge of
the shape under and behind.
This flap weights the front
edge of the flying wing.

7 Crease the shape along the
vertical midline, but do not
leave it folded. This reinforces
the crease made in step 2
and will make it easier for you
to do the folds in step 8.

8 Crease to both the left and
right of the vertical midline.
Fold up from the middle
crease, then fold the creases
down on either side to create
a fuselage with wings.

9 You can now fly the glider;
be sure to hold it from the tail
end, with the wings forward.
You may need to experiment
with how you hold it and how
you angle the wings.

17

scheduling classes

We teachers found Post-it® Notes to be the perfect solution for scheduling classes at our high school. We write every class on a color-coded note and stick the notes on the chalkboard. Each teacher in turn takes a note and puts it on his or her calendar; then we repeat this until we've taken all the notes. What would otherwise be a lengthy and laborious task is completed in minutes.

Sarah P., Oakland, CA

18

organizing lab worksheets

I use three-ring binders to organize the worksheets and other information for each of the science units that I teach. After completing a lesson or lab session, I stick the worksheets (master and answer key) back into the binder along with a Post-it® Note that summarizes how the lesson worked, how much time it took, and the changes that I need to make for the following year. During the summer recess, I review my notes and make any necessary revisions. Because I've already organized all the units, I can easily add any new material or ideas that I generate.

Tracey T., Havana, IL

19

sticking to the (lesson) plan

As a teacher, I love using Post-it® Notes in my lesson-plan book. They allow me to make quick and easy changes to the schedule without rewriting the same information again and again. When I have to repeat lessons, I can move them to the next day with very little effort.

Heidi R., Windsor, MO

20

a chorus of approval

As a choir conductor, I spend hours preparing detailed notes for an upcoming rehearsal. Post-it® Notes are perfect for this! Gone are the days of erasing notations in my score. The feeling of satisfaction I get from hurling a note into the air after successfully rehearsing a difficult section is indescribable. As the rehearsal unfolds, I celebrate progress with a confetti-like exuberance of notes in the air.

Harry C., Castro Valley, CA

21

singing praises

When I perform at church on Sunday mornings, I find Post-it® Notes to be invaluable. They help me find and play the right music at the correct time in the service. I write "Prelude," "Communion," and so forth on notes, then stick each note on the appropriate piece. I use them over and over and store them in my hymnals.

Marylinn W., Sisters, OR

22 classroom seating charts

To make a seating chart for each of the classes I teach, I copy a blank template of the classroom's desk arrangement. I put each student's name on a Post-it® Note and place the note in the box that denotes the correct desk. Whenever I need to move a student, I can quickly and easily reposition the notes. Also, when a student has dropped a class or moved to a different class period, I place his or her Post-it® Note on a reminder card to move the grade information and other materials to the new class or to take them out altogether.

Rene B., Anaheim, CA

23

ahh, yes, a little to the left...

You may think this sounds nuts, but we use Post-it® Notes to tag muscle groups on horses. As equine massage therapists, we run how-to clinics where owners can learn basic massage for their horses. During the classroom session, we stick notes labeled with the major muscle groups under discussion on both sides of a horse. The notes stay on the entire time we are discussing the muscle groups and do not disturb the horse at all, as other types of labels are likely to do.

Halide C., Guilford, CT

creating

"Everything you can imagine is real," observed famed artist Pablo Picasso. Whether you're helping your kid with a crafts project or sitting down to paint a portrait, creativity occurs when you set your imagination free. And art doesn't require working on canvas or in marble. A satisfying creative act can be as simple as folding pieces of paper and letting your dreams take flight.

the art of playing

Just because you're a grown-up doesn't mean you can't play! Find a creative activity you enjoy and build time for it into your schedule, even if it's just an hour or two on a weekend. You'll feel as refreshed as if you've had a mini-vacation.

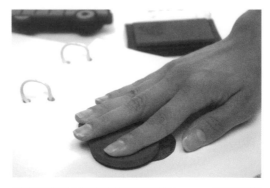

24

stamp art

I use Post-it® Notes all the time for rubber-stamping projects. First, I stamp a note and cut the stamped shape out to make a mask. I then use the note several times, positioning it under the stamp so it masks out sections of the surface and creates a unique layered effect. I can't imagine stamping without Post-it® Notes!

Laurie J., New London, OH

Artwork by Dax Morrison

25 mini flip books

I make flip books out of pads of Post-it® Notes, then give them away as fun little gifts.

Karen R., Vancouver, WA

26

painless paint masking

As a do-it-yourself enthusiast, I've found Post-it® Notes useful for many projects. For example, before painting in tight corners or around small areas, such as switch plates, heater ducts, or baseboards, I mask them with notes. Cleanup is almost instant!

Paul K., Portland, OR

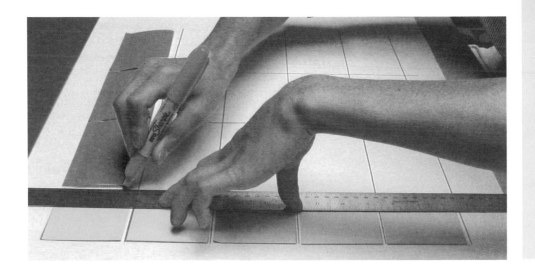

27

marking chart grids

Post it® Notes make setting up charts quick and easy. First I choose a note with the size I need for columns and rows, and then I mark off the grid one line at a time, either moving the first note as I go along or adding more. I draw in the lines (using a ruler to make sure that I draw them straight), then peel off the notes.

Friedrich K., Potsdam, Germany

28

artist's assistant

I paint custom landscapes and frequently use Post-it® Notes to make a guide for a straight line. They are quick to put in place, keep an awesome straight edge, can be reused several times, and peel off in a snap.

Vicki L., New Prague, MN

from note to building

29

I am an architect specializing in a combination of traditional Caribbean and modern architecture. In the early phases of a new project, I sketch my ideas on Post it® Notes using typical office supplies: I "paint" the walls with white correctional fluid, the sea with a marker, and the red sunset skies with architectural markup pens. I then re-create them at a larger size either as an acrylic painting on canvas or as a giclée print. The process quite literally goes from Post-It® Note to painting to architectural plan—and at the end, my creation finally becomes a building.

Pedro T., Grand Cayman, Cayman Islands

30 noteworthy art

I used hundreds of Post-it® Notes in an installation selected by the Austin Museum of Art in Texas to be in its "New Art in Austin" exhibition. I stuck die-cut and numbered Post-it® Notes to a wall as "leaves" on a painted tree trunk. Other notes were scattered on the floor, and viewers of my work were encouraged to take them home as a memento.

Hunter C., Austin, TX

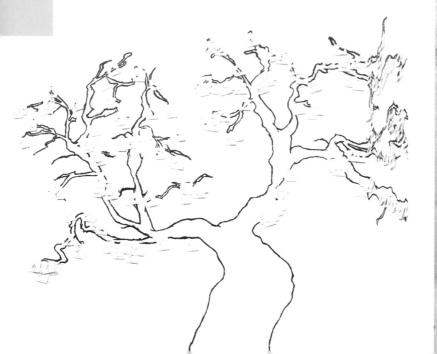

note-ably artistic!

Since 2004, 3M Canada has sponsored the Note-able Art Competition, first in Ontario and then in Québec. Throughout this book, you'll find the inspired and incredibly inventive works submitted by Canadian art students.

grand-prize winner!

Contestants were required to submit an original work of art, composed primarily of Post-it® Notes, no larger than one square meter each. Below is the winning entry from the 2004 competition, entitled *The Bustier,* by Jane Kline of the Toronto School of Art. Congratulations, Jane!

Artwork by Jane Kline

setting records

A Post-it® Note featuring a drawing by artist R.B. Kitaj sold for $925 during an online auction for charity in 2000, creating a Guinness World Record for the most valuable Post-it® Note.

Artwork by (clockwise from top left)
Ann Hobday, Joseph Sesito, Janelle Dubeau,
Lisa Vanderwoude, Valerie Marchand, and Pei-shan Chai

organizing small parts

I use Post-it® Notes to label parts and their sizes or quantities for my woodworking projects. This system helps me keep various parts organized and ensures that I have all the parts I need before I start a new project.

Glenn S., Bakersfield, CA

33

purls of wisdom

As a novice knitter, I use Post-it® Notes to help me keep track of which row I am knitting. When I have to knit a particular number of rows, I keep a tally right on a note—that way my pattern stays clean. The notes also show me if I should be doing a knit stitch or a purl stitch, so I avoid having to fix mistakes.

Stacy N., Federal Way, WA

34

christmas countdown

We like to use Post-it® Notes during the Christmas holidays. They are great for making easy peel-off Advent calendars, even the children can help! We also enjoy creating colorful paper garlands for the tree using Post-it® Pop-up Notes.

Lars L., Oslo, Norway

encouraging
the born artist

Children are instinctively creative
and see the world through fresh
eyes, without preconceptions or
limits. Foster your kids' artistic
expression by giving them materials
that let them explore color and
shape to their hearts' content.

35

capture the flag

Post-it® Notes make great toy flags. Here's how: orient the note so the adhesive side is on the left. Place a craft stick on the adhesive strip, halfway up the note. Now fold down the note in half over the stick, and press the two sides' adhesive strips firmly together. To make more-complex flags, stick on strips and shapes cut from colored notes. Decorate with stickers and colored markers—then get ready to storm the castle!

Judy B., Boca Raton, FL

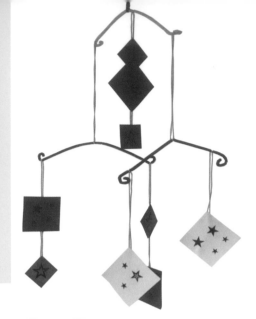

37

easy découpage

I use Post-it® Notes for simple découpage projects with my kids. We cover almost anything—including glass votives, wooden picture frames, and vases—with bright notes. This is a quick and easy project to complete—even for small hands and short attention spans.

Helen R., Macon, GA

36

baby mobile

Keep your baby entertained during diaper changes with a colorful mobile made from Post-it® Notes. Using pipe cleaners and strong thread or yarn, stick notes back to back in an arrangement that is as large and ornate or as small and simple as you wish. (Never hang the mobile over the baby's crib where it could pose a choking hazard.)

Anne-Sophie M., Marseille, France

38

notable costumes

Post-it® Notes can help you make creative Halloween costumes. Make a dinosaur by covering an oversized T-shirt with green notes (Post-it® Super Sticky Notes work best) and place pink or yellow ones along the back for spikes or spots!

Aleksander A., Syosset, NY

39

robot bookmark

I enjoy making these robot bookmarks with my children. We stick small Post-it® Notes onto larger ones, then fold long, narrow notes into accordion folds to give movement to the neck and limbs. The kids put on the finishing touches with stickers and stamps.

Debbie M., Sydney, Australia

40

eggstra fun

At Easter time, we make big, colorful "eggs" by placing Post-it® Notes on balloons. Each child picks a different color palette so they don't get mixed up. Even our two-year-old can easily peel off and stick on notes. After all the notes are on, the bigger kids brush them with découpage sealer, creating a shell somewhat like papier-mâché. When the sealer is dry, the kids pop the balloons, leaving a shell made of sealed notes. Voilà! They have bright, cheerful decorations perfect for their rooms.

Angie W., Andersen AFB, Guam

41

homemade piñata

Our family created a fabulous piñata for my son's birthday party. After stuffing candy and other goodies inside a small cardboard box, we decorated the outside of the box with Post-it® Notes. It was a great family project, and as a result my son was much more interested in it than he would have been in a store-bought piñata. Because kids usually get excited only after the piñata finally breaks open, an unexpected bonus was the excitement they got from seeing all the notes sent flying with every whack.

Heather B., San Francisco, CA

build a piñata!

- find a cardboard box
- load it with goodies
- tape it loosely shut
- layer Post-it® Notes all over the box
- add ears and eyes if desired
- hang it in an open space
- stand back and watch the fun!

planning

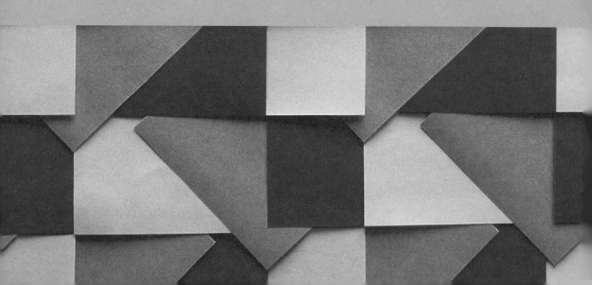

"Let our advance worrying become advance thinking and planning," advised Sir Winston Churchill. All too often, it is easy to waste time and energy fretting about the challenges ahead—whether you are planning for a happy occasion or simply dealing with everyday details. How much better it would be to transform unproductive worrying into organized thinking and planning.

taking the long view

Once you've set a big goal for yourself, break it down into small, achievable tasks, each with its own reasonable deadline. Don't worry about that daunting goal. Just take it one small step at a time—you'll be done before you know it.

42

long-range planning

My fiancée and I were planning a number of major events—a wedding, a construction project, several trips, and the launch of a new business—in the same six-month period. To make sure nothing slipped through the cracks, we knew we had to keep all the components for each project visible. I divided a Post-it® Easel Pad by project and by month, and listed everything we needed to do in the appropriate time slot. We wrote action items on Post-it® Notes so we could grab them and go. When new tasks came up, we wrote them on separate notes and then put them onto the chart. This system made a crazy period in our lives much less daunting.

Gordon S., Vancouver, Canada

43 scheduling shortcuts

Instead of writing down (and changing and rearranging) regularly scheduled meetings or tasks in my planner week after week, month after month, I use Post-it® Notes to simplify matters. I write each task or meeting on its own note and place it in my planner on the appropriate date. When I complete the task or finish the meeting, I move the note to the next due date. I also color-code the notes—blue for weekly, green for monthly, and yellow for quarterly. Post-it® Notes save me lots of time!

Sandy S., Union City, OK

planning a party

Shake, rattle, and roll—it's party time! Whether you're firing up the grill for friends or planning a fête for 50, throwing a successful party requires a little panache and plenty of planning. Both are easy to do with the help of Post-it® Notes.

44

easy seating plan

We enjoy giving dinner parties but dread arranging the seating. Using Post-it® Notes makes the task so much easier. We write each person's name on a note. We use blue notes for male guests and pink notes for female ones. Then we swap guests' names around the tables on paper until we find the best combination. It certainly beats erasing and rewriting names!

Freya W., Terrey Hills, Australia

Susie
• chatty
• divorced
• bringing wine

Evan
• newly single
• drinks!
• leaving early

Diane
• horse vet
• interested in Carlos?

Carlos
• used to ride
• South Beach
• hates smoke

Martin

Table #1

Me

Rachel
• allergic to cilantro
• Spain?

Gabe
• trip to Spain
• available??
• NO political talk

Lisa
• ACLU work
• coming late
• vegetarian

James
• smokes
• drinks!!
• bad jokes!

45

buffet strategy

When I'm preparing for a holiday party, I set out all the serving dishes in position on my kitchen island, which functions as a buffet. On Post-it® Notes, I list all the food items, one per note, that I plan to serve, then place each note by its dish. This prevents my discovering an unserved side dish in the fridge the day after the event.

Juli S., Santa Barbara, CA

46

dishing it up

Before a dinner party, I lay out my serving baskets, dishes, and platters, and label them with Post-it® Notes: crostini, crackers, asparagus, spaghetti, and so on. That way, I know at a glance which platter or bowl will hold which food, so I can make sure there are enough for all the items I plan to serve.

Lenore N., San Francisco, CA

47

perfect wine pairing

We're wine connoisseurs who love to throw multicourse dinners that highlight the characteristics of different wines. When meal preparations are going full-throttle, though, keeping track of the wines themselves can really get chaotic. To make order from this chaos, we number a series of Post-it® Notes and stick them to toothpicks pushed directly into the bottle corks in the order they'll be served. We stick a duplicate set of notes—which also includes the name of the dish that each wine is paired with—in a row along the edge of a cupboard, just above where we serve the food.

Elizabeth B., New York, NY

48

keeping tabs on your drink

There have been so many times that I've forgotten which glass was mine at a party. I've solved this problem when I host parties by placing a pad of Post-it® Notes and a pen on the bar. The guests write their names on notes, which they can then stick on the base of their glasses.

Giacomo G., Viareggio, Italy

49

impromptu place cards

As we throw lots of casual dinner parties, we came up with a no-fuss idea for place cards using Post-it® Notes. I take a pad of notes (adhesive edge facing me and at the bottom), and write a name on the lower half of each note, between the center and the adhesive. I then fold the note in half above the name, creating a tent card. I then fold the top and bottom halves inward again and tuck one section inside, forming a triangle with a stable base. The sticky strip holds the overlapping edges together.

Remy P., Montréal, Canada

50

color-coding cookbooks

I use Post-it® Notes to color-code my cookbooks—using different colors for each course (main dishes are blue, for example). Each recipe I'd like to try is flagged with a note outlining how much time is required to prepare it.

Melinda M., Manassas, VA

51

party countdown

I'm not naturally at ease entertaining, so when I do throw a party, preparation is key. I make a master list of everything that needs to get done: shopping, cleaning, setting up, and cooking. That main list gets broken down into smaller lists on Post-it® Notes that I pass out to my husband and kids. Cooking has the greatest potential for disaster so, after choosing a menu from my cookbooks, I write down what I need to do for each dish, how long each step takes, and when I need to do it on a large note stuck to the fridge: "Two days ahead—brine the turkey," "One day ahead—shop, buy flowers, roast vegetables for soup," and so on. My countdown lists give me peace of mind, knowing everything is accounted for.

Olivia M., Normandy, France

Artwork by Tara Mulcahey

52

great icebreaker

I use this great game to help guests who don't know each other mingle more easily. Before the party, I write the names of celebrities, historical figures, or fictional characters on Post-it® Notes. As guests arrive, I stick a note to each person's back or hair. They then have to roam around and ask each other for clues—"Am I famous?" "Am I a scientist?" "Am I dead?"—until each guest discovers his or her secret identity.

Lisa M., Tulsa, OK

Prince Charles

Katharine Hepburn

Marquis de Sade

Homer Simpson

Mahatma Gandhi

Babe Ruth

Mickey Mouse

Eleanor Roosevelt

53

congratulatory banner

I love making banners for any celebration: birthdays, anniversaries, awards, or new babies. I write out the message twice, letter by letter, on differently colored Post-it® Notes. Sticking the adhesive strips together, I pair up the first and last letters, the second and next-to-last, and so on. I then hang the paired notes over a string or ribbon that I suspend between walls.

Claudia L., Toulouse, France

54

last-minute streamers

It was a coworker's birthday, and we didn't have any decorations. We took a pad of Post-it® Pop-up Notes, unfurled them, and strung them around her cubicle before she arrived at work. They looked just like streamers.

Christy M., Elizabeth, NJ

55

work-themed parties

Some companies I work with prefer not to celebrate traditional holidays. I like to suggest that they celebrate days that relate to the workplace. One of the most popular is the birthday of Post-it® Notes. April 6th is a great day for a cheery party to move folks out of lingering winter doldrums and into springtime. I've even heard of cakes decorated to look like Post-it® Notes!

Patt S., Seattle, WA

56

office high jinks

You may think we have too much time on our hands, but this was a prank we pulled on a favorite coworker. He loved it!

Damon E., Vancouver, Canada

planning a wedding

For many people, no life event seems more hectic to plan than a wedding. With so many big and small details to attend to, it's helpful to come up with a system to let you make order out of chaos—and let you truly enjoy the best day of your life.

Uncle Charlie

Anne Carter

57

wedding-bell blues (and yellows)

When our son was getting married, I was trying desperately to figure out a way to organize seating for more than 300 people at the reception. I bought several differently colored pads of small Post-it® Notes. As each RSVP came in, I wrote the guest's name on a single note. All of the groom's relatives were recorded on blue notes, and the bride's were written on magenta notes. The groom's friends were on green notes, the bride's on yellow notes, and so on. On a sheet of poster paper, I drew large circles to represent tables of eight, then I stuck the individual notes around each table. It was very easy to move the names around, and the colors helped me ensure that each table had the right mix of people.

Ellen E., Chevy Chase, MD

58

song cues

On Post-it® Notes, we wrote the name of each song we wanted the band to play during our wedding reception, along with any special instructions, such as when to play the first dance. This helped the band organize its playlist and ensured that the entertainment flowed smoothly.

Anat S., Tel Aviv, Israel

59

budgeting nuptials

When we were getting married, it seemed like every day new expenses came up that we had to track. We wrote each item, its cost, and the vendor's phone number on a separate Post-it® Note, then stuck it on a blank page in our wedding binder. I assigned a different color for each category—caterer, photographer, minister, and so on. If we later found a better deal, we'd just add a new note, and we recorded regular budget updates on fresh notes. The wedding came in on budget!

Mary H., Galway, Ireland

60

automatic thank-yous

When opening our wedding presents, my wife and I kept a pad of Post-it® Notes handy. We'd write the name of the giver and comments about the gift, including our first happy reaction, on a note and tuck it inside the card that came with the gift. We also tore out the envelope's return address and stuck it partway under the note's adhesive strip so it wouldn't fall out. When it came time to say thanks to everyone, we pulled out the cards, and the thank-you notes practically wrote themselves.

Don V., Richmond Hill, Canada

soul mate sticks!

A woman found her soul mate thanks to a Post-it® Note. After she scribbled her number on a note, her now-husband stuck it on his desk and forgot about it. Weeks passed, but the note stuck around until finally he asked her out. Their relationship stuck, and a year later personalized Post-it® Note favors accompanied their wedding invitations.

moving to new digs

Moving can be a time of major joy—and trauma! To ensure that all goes smoothly, start planning your move as far in advance as possible. Post-it® Notes are a mover's natural ally and will help you make sure nothing slips through the cracks.

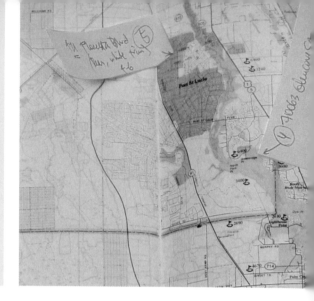

61

open-house itinerary

When house-hunting, there can be so many places to see in a short time period that if you haven't got your open-house route mapped out, you can miss half of them by getting lost. With the newspaper listings and a street map in hand, I write down the address and hours of each open house on a Post-it® Note. I draw an arrow to a corner of the note, along with the order of the houses I want to visit, and then stick the note on the destination. Even though the map is covered in notes, I can still see the best route to get to each house on time.

Danelle M., San Francisco, CA

circle the world

Based on the size of Earth's circumference of about 25,000 miles and using three-inch-square Post-it® Notes, it would take more than half a billion notes to circle the world once around!

62

sorting computer cables

I use Post-it® Notes to label cables connected to the backs of TVs, DVD players, stereos, and PCs. On each note, I write what each cable is attached to, then fold the note around the cable so it sticks to itself. The notes make it easier to troubleshoot connections and hook things up again if I have to unplug them.

Ken B., San Jose, CA

63

hot tip for movers

Here's a trick I've passed on to many friends who were moving to new homes: before you unpack the kitchen boxes, take a pad of Post-it® Notes labeled with "glasses," "pots," "baking goods," and so on. Now walk through a few typical activities, such as making dinner. Where do you need to have your cooking utensils so that you can quickly grab them? Put the note labeled "utensils" on that drawer. Continue attaching notes to the outside of the cabinets and drawers that make the most sense for cooking. Then think through another kitchen activity, such as emptying the dishwasher. It's easy to see if something is awkwardly placed. Moving notes is so much easier than rearranging your kitchen, and it saves you time and energy at a time when you least have it.

Brulene Z., Roseville, CA

64 moving furnishings

When I plan a move, I use Post-it® Notes to label and color-code by room each piece of furniture and decorative item. When the movers arrive, the colors of the notes tell them where to deliver each item. (I also indicate which room is which in the new house with color-coordinated notes stuck on the doors.) You can use the same strategy when staging or redecorating a home.

Kimberly M., Peterborough, NH

gardening

Mother Nature doesn't label growing things, but people often need to. One key to nurturing your own patch of earth successfully is keeping records and reminders of your garden plans and plant lists tucked away indoors. That'll save you from having to guess!

65

watering plants

I have a device that tests the moisture in the soil of potted plants. My six-year-old grandson likes to use it to see which plants need watering, and he's disappointed when I can't follow him immediately with the watering can. So I give him a pad of Post-it® Notes. He sticks a note on each thirsty plant. Later, I water the plants he's marked, removing the notes as I go. My grandson is happy that he's been so helpful—and my plants are happy, too.

Kate B., Ada, MI

66

seed saviors

Post-it® Notes do double duty on my collection of seed packets. I stick a note on each one indicating where I've planted those particular seeds, together with planting information. Then I efficiently reseal the packet with the adhesive strip so I don't lose any seeds.

Virginia S., Norwich, England

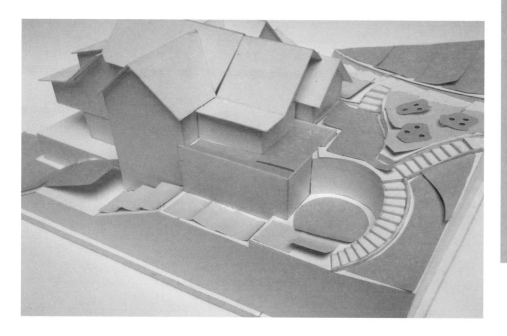

67

planning a garden

We made a simple model of our house and used Post-it® Notes
to plan the landscaping. We cut shapes out of differently colored
notes to represent different plants. Then we arranged the shapes
around the model until we were satisfied with the placement of
each bed and tree. Since we could also write down sun and water
requirements right on the notes, we could double-check that the
soil conditions were suitable before we dug any holes.

Colleen W, Sydney, Australia

brainstorming

"Genius is one percent inspiration and 99 percent perspiration," said inventor Thomas Edison. Whether you are tackling a problem on your own or with a group, the trick is to generate an avalanche of ideas. It's important to bring in a fresh perspective, and have some fun, too. Playfully throwing out a wealth of ideas tends to be more productive—and creative—than focusing solely on serious solutions.

the art of brainstorming

Metaphorically speaking, great ideas come in all sizes, colors, and shapes, just like Post-it® Notes. When you're brainstorming, use this similarity to your advantage, letting different types of notes spark ideas that can be literally off the wall!

68

calling all ideas

As a facilitator, I use Post-It® Notes as a brainstorming tool. Each member of the brainstorming session gets a pad of notes. Then we take a few minutes to write down ideas, one per note. Afterward, we post the notes in front of the room on a whiteboard or flip chart. We then identify ideas that share common concepts and put these notes together. This approach encourages everyone to come up with ideas and then discuss them freely. It also clearly shows when individuals are thinking along similar lines while identifying unusual or unique ideas. Perhaps the best benefit is that everyone's contribution is valued.

Helena W., Castro Valley, CA

try peer reviews

69

brainstorming note by note

The art of brainstorming comes down to two things. First, make it easy to express and share ideas. Second, make it easy to connect the dots, so the bigger picture emerges from all the individual ideas. In my work as a consultant, my clients and I write every idea we can think of, no matter how crazy it might seem, on a Post-it® Note. We then organize them into categories using a Post-it® Easel Pad, so it's easy to create sheets for each topic. That in turn makes it easy for me to break the participants into smaller groups who can then replicate this process for their designated topics. I repeat this process for as many levels of analysis that each topic warrants, then bring the group back together so they see everything.

William B., Pasadena, CA

70

flowcharting

We use Post-it® Notes to create flowcharts on the wall, whether we're analyzing existing business procedures or mapping out the most efficient way to proceed on a new project. We employ different colors to represent different team members or departments.

Steve R., Grants Pass, OR

71

color-coded planning

To form the basis for my planning of any project or proposal, I first place a large Post-it® Self-Stick Table Top Pad on my desk. Then I write the central idea on a mid-sized Post-it® Note and put it in the center of the pad's sheet. Next, I draw lines out from the central idea for each of the main tracks of my project—for example, the separate chapters of a book. Next, I write the central idea for each track or chapter on smaller, different-color notes, and stick them at the other end of each line. Finally, when the brainstorm subsides, I have a useful visual of what topics I will cover, and I am free to add ideas or move things around without having to rewrite anything.

Bette D., Pleasanton, CA

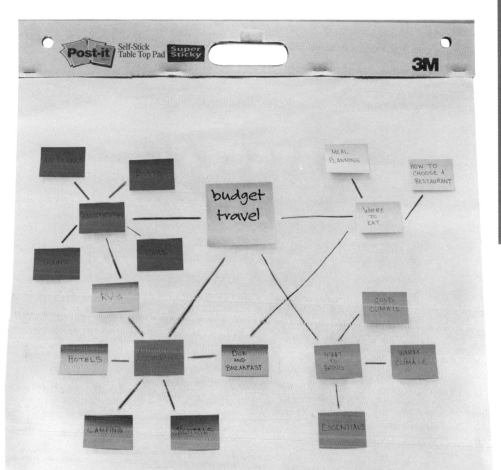

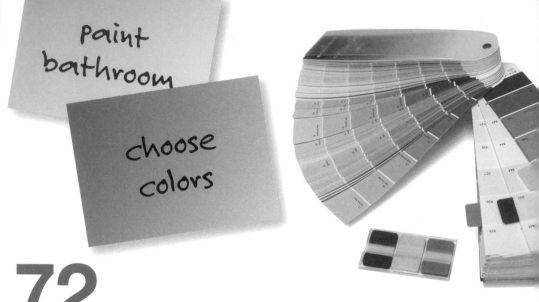

72

breaking down a project

As a consultant, I teach my clients to consider every single little task necessary to accomplish a particular goal, whether it's painting a room, planning a vacation, changing jobs, or starting a business. First, write each task on its own Post-it® Note. Then, working backward from the goal, organize the notes on a large surface, repeatedly asking yourself, "What needs to be done before this task can be completed?" Place tasks that need to be executed simultaneously in columns, and place those to be done sequentially in rows. Once the project is laid out, add dates and designate who is responsible for each item. As each task is completed, move its note to an area labeled "completed" so you can quickly see your progress.

Laurie W., Littleton, CO

73

remodeling resources

Before remodeling our house last year, I flipped through magazines for ideas. I used a differently colored Post-it® Note to tag ideas for each room: blue for the master bedroom, yellow for the kids' rooms, green for the kitchen, pink for bathrooms, and so on. My partner and I then culled the ideas down to those we really liked, tore them out, and filed them in binders by room.

Deepak R., Windsor, Canada

think outside the box

Not only are Post-it® Notes great facilitators for brainstorming, they can also be used to solve those pesky issues that keep coming up. Brainstorm a bit to see how you can take advantage of the notes' versatility in unexpected ways.

74

blinded by the light

The digital clock in our bedroom has a display that is backlit in a very intense shade of blue. My husband says the light is too bright for him to sleep. He had been covering the display with an ugly T-shirt to block out the light. The other day I noticed that the offending light was discreetly covered with a Post-it® Note, which Mr. Sensitive Eyes peels off in the morning and puts back each night. Much nicer than the shirt!

Lisa B., Little Rock, AR

75

check, please

My friend keeps a pad of small Post-it® Notes in her purse. When dining out with a group of people who want to pay separately, she pulls out her pad. Everyone's credit card gets its own note, and all the diners write down how much the server should charge each card.

Meg O., Salem, MA

76

hanging without hang-ups

When we are hanging heavy framed art, my husband and I use Post-it® Notes to mark the locations of the wall studs, where the nails will go. We put an *X* on each note to mark the spot, so we don't write directly on the wall. We then use separate notes to show where we want to place the top edge of the frames.

Monica C., Fitchburg, WI

77

police notes

At the police station, we receive thousands of traffic complaints. Our traffic unit uses Post-it® Notes to inform citizens that a deputy has been in their neighborhood addressing their complaint. Now we've expanded the practice. When detectives are canvassing a neighborhood to gather information following a crime, they write their contact information on notes and stick them to doors, asking residents to call if they can contribute any leads.

David B., Deltona, FL

78

undercover slot machines

My mother-in-law takes Post-it® Notes with her to the casino to cover up the payout line on a slot machine! She doesn't want to see what comes up after each pull of the lever or push of the button. She just waits to collect her winnings.

Stephanie C., Gold River, CA

79

elevator opener

The elevator to our condo has a sensor that opens the door if anything passes in front of it. We keep a Post-it® Note stuck to the inside wall of the elevator. When we want to hold the door open to load or unload, we simply place the note over the sensor. Who knows how many years old this one note is!

Angela G., Redondo Beach, CA

fun fact

Faced with the last-minute task of decorating the "just married" car at a friend's wedding—and no cans in sight—an Iowa woman got creative. Grabbing a pack of multicolored Post-it® Notes, she stuck them all over the car. It was a big hit at the reception!

80   just-in-case addresses

When mailing an important package, I write a copy
of the address on a Post-it® Note and put it inside.
If the address on the outside of the package
becomes illegible, there's a backup address inside.

Leslie H., Jersey City, NJ

81   poster roller

When I can't find a rubber band, I use
a Post-it® Note to keep a poster rolled
up for storage or transport. It's strong
enough to hold the poster in place, and
it doesn't mark or wrinkle the paper.

Paul K., Portland, OR

the silver arrows
of level nine are
up two screens
and left one.

the third
heart container is
in the desert

82

video game navigation

In the original *The Legend of Zelda*® video game, players must navigate a series of complex dungeons, collecting items along the way in a specific order. After I had navigated three of the nine levels, I started getting lost. So I used Post-it® Notes to record where I'd been and to piece together a five-by-nine-foot map of the dungeons on the wall above the TV to keep it all straight.

Patricia S., Berkeley Heights, NJ

83

labeling recycled bottles

I wash out vitamin bottles and reuse them as containers for individual servings of homemade salad dressings that I bring to work for lunch each day. Post-it® Notes make ideal labels for these containers.

Leslie H., Jersey City, NJ

hold that thought

"Memory," noted Irish playwright Oscar Wilde, "is the diary that we all carry about with us." Alas, some of us are better than others at keeping our mental diaries up-to-date. The trick is developing a system for remembering things that would otherwise get lost: birthdays, meetings, chores, or even sudden flashes of inspiration. One solution always works, as a writer like Wilde knew: jot it down!

remembering

Life runs at such a breakneck pace, it's a wonder we don't forget half of what we need to do. How to remember it all? Keep a pen and a pad of Post-it® Notes handy to capture those flashes of brilliance (or simply your shopping list) and set your mind at rest.

84

ideas everywhere

I place a pad of Post-it® Notes in my pocket every morning. During the day, when an idea springs up for a client, an article, or my book, I quickly record the thought on a note and stick it to the back of the pad. Later, I move each note to the place where action needs to happen: book ideas go into that book's binder, client ideas onto my monitor, and errands onto the front door. I don't miss much! I do all of this neatly, so my home doesn't look like a crazy person lives there.

Else T., St. Paul, MN

85

wear your heart on your sleeve

I sometimes put a Post-it® Note on my sleeve when I have too many things on my mind and I don't want to forget something important. "Anniversary tomorrow!" is a good example.

Carol B., Alamo, CA

86

ideas on the march

My best thinking happens while I'm walking, so a pad of Post-it® Notes and a golf pencil in my fanny pack allow me to capture ideas while I'm on the go. When a thought comes, I write it on a note, then stick it on the front of my jacket. Once I'm home, I pull the notes off and get ready to work. I have been doing this for more than 15 years.

Janie J., Victoria, MN

87

nighttime idea capture

I keep Post-it® Notes by my bed. When it's quiet at night, I always end up remembering something I need to do. Now I write it on a note so I can forget it, turn over, and go to sleep.

Nancy G., Columbus, GA

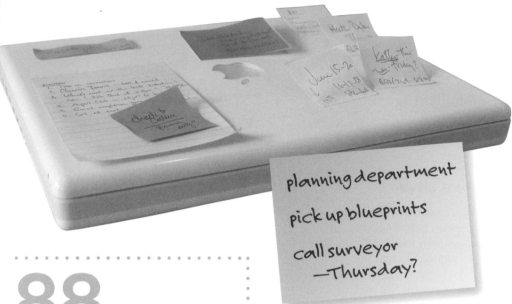

planning department

pick up blueprints

call surveyor
—Thursday?

88

on-screen callbacks

When I'm on the phone and another client calls, I write their information on a Post-it® Note so I can call them back. Then I stick it on the middle of my computer screen where I'll be sure to see it. In the past, I've forgotten that a person has called, or I've written it down but didn't see it because the note wasn't obvious. Now it is.

Sheila M., Upland, CA

89

laptop to-do lists

I've stumbled on the perfect solution to my daily chaos: I write my to-do lists on Post-it® Notes and stick them to my laptop. After I check my email in the morning, I peel them off and hit the road with my trusty collection of reminders!

Caroline L., Glasgow, Scotland

90

lawn saver

I'm a professional organizer with attention deficit disorder, so I constantly forget things. Last year, I forgot to turn the automatic sprinklers for our garden back on after it rained, and we soon had a very dead lawn. As a result, I've learned to put a Post-it® Note on the door leading to the garage (and my car) that reminds me, "Water is off."

Sheila M., Upland, CA

92

family statistics

Ever gone clothes shopping and been unable to remember someone's size? Record each family member's clothing and shoe sizes on a separate Post-it® Note, and stick it on a dedicated page in your day planner. Update the sizes as your children grow, or after a family member has been on a diet.

Tomoyo M., Hilo, HI

91

remembering birthdays

Forgetting your grandchildren's birthdays will be a thing of the past if you jot down the dates on Post-it® Notes. Write each name and date on a separate note. Stick them in your calendar or day planner one week ahead of the date to alert you to buy a gift or card in time. Next year, just move the reminder notes to your new calendar, and start the process anew.

Maria Julia S., Coyoacán, Mexico

93

no more senior moments

For we seniors and our "senior moments," Post-it® Notes are excellent. I stick them on my calendar as "ticklers," so I always remember certain events or chores each week or month. They are so handy! It is hard to remember what my life was like before Post-it® Notes.

Marylinn W., Sisters, OR

94 daily schedule on display

Busy, independent senior citizens like us often have many appointments to juggle and remember. My husband and I have perfected a reminder system using Post-it® Notes. Each morning we neatly stick three rows of notes on a cabinet above the toaster, informing us of upcoming activities. Color-coded by "his," "hers," and "ours," the notes are arranged chronologically. No more memory lapses: now, my husband and I are instantly aware of each other's schedules. Our system makes life easier, and we've earned a reputation for being dependable and having exceptional memories. Thank you, Post-it® Notes, for making the golden years easier.

Shirley K., Coral Springs, FL

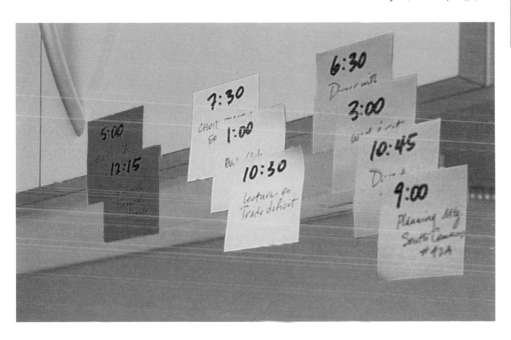

95

project markers

I use Post-it® Notes to jot reminders of where I've left off in a large project. That way, I can get right back on track without spending extra time trying to familiarize myself with a task after an interruption.

Tina M., Merrill, WI

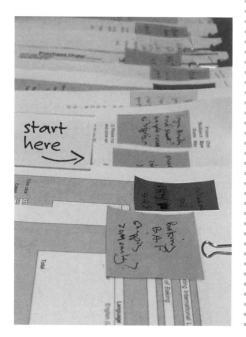

96

well-framed thoughts

I stick reminders jotted on Post-it® Notes onto my computer monitor's frame when my desk is a mess, so they stay visible.

Julie H., Oakland, CA

97

remembering clients

I stick a chunk of Post-it® Notes in the back of my calendar or in the notebook that's always with me for times when I want to write a quick note to a client or colleague while I'm away from my desk

Kathleen P., Itasca, IL

readers' aids

Necessity is the mother of invention. The simple need for a bookmark that didn't fall out of a hymnal gave birth to the original Post-it® Note. Bookmarking is still one of their most popular uses. Keep a few notes handy for marking favorite passages.

98

preaching to the choir

Members of our choir use Post-it® Notes to mark the songs for mass each week. That way we don't have to leaf through our hymnals or get distracted by bookmarks falling out. It works like a charm! How did we ever get along without Post-it® Notes?

Elisa S., Glenmoore, PA

99

tenacious bookmarks

I use Post-it® Notes as bookmarks. They don't fall out easily, even if you drop the book. And if I want to comment on something that I'm reading, I can jot down my thoughts right there and then.

Tina M., Merrill, WI

100

book club thoughts

While the other members of my book club work from memory, or underline or highlight important points, I, having the poorest memory, use Post-it® Notes to keep track of my comments. At the meetings, I am often teased about the number of notes poking out from the top, side, and bottom of my book. Color, size, and shape don't matter—I always have the notes. (In fact, guess what I got the members of my book club for Christmas? They were thrilled—all teasing aside.)

Patti C., Monona, WI

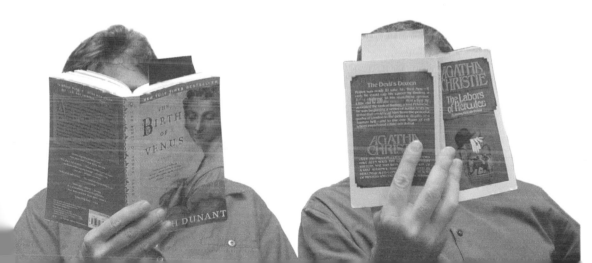

managing
time

"I wasted time," lamented Shakespeare's King Richard II, "and now doth time waste me." All too often, time seems like a commodity that keeps slipping away. But if you treat time as money, budgeting it just as you would dollars and cents, you can use it more effectively. Create a time budget for any task on your to-do list and see how spending time wisely will pay off big-time.

making a run for the money

Exploring a large city for the first time? Or just running errands in your hometown? Your dashboard or steering wheel is the perfect place to plot your course of action with Post-it® Notes—while keeping your eye on the road, of course!

101

challah run

With a toddler in tow and another baby on the way, my memory often does not serve me well. So every Friday, I place a Post-it® Note on the steering wheel of my car that says, "Don't forget to pick up challah!" This is the only way I can be sure to have the bread, an important part of our Shabbat meal, on the table.

Chalyn N., Albany, CA

102

driving notes

I keep a steady supply of Post-it® Notes in my car, since I always seem to be on the go—for work, for errands, or for the kids' activities. Every morning, I stick a note right onto my steering wheel with reminders of errands that I have to do that day. Then I stick on a second note with shopping lists, making it easy to peel off and go.

Lisa L., Guilford, CT

hardware store

- new showerhead
- extension cord
- rose food
- check on window order

103

cure for the hopelessly lost

I'm not very good at finding my way around, particularly when I'm going to a place I've never been. That's why I write the directions I need in large print on a Post-it® Note and stick it right in front of me on the steering wheel. Sometimes I even draw a simplified map on the note, so I can get where I'm going without having to take my eyes off the road to search the car for a map.

Ines C., Phoenix, AZ

Dwight to 6th
rt 2 miles
Turn left at 2nd
traffic light
(x-st is Elm)
1447 6th

104

driving directions for firefighters

I work for a small fire department. We use a carbon-copy form to write down the address and nature of each call we get. We ran out of response forms once, so I put the necessary information on Post-it® Notes. They worked great. I stuck a note with the address on the truck's dashboard so the whole crew could see where they were going.

Cheri E., Eastlake, OH

pick up Noah — 2 pm
Cordonices Park
1844 Euclid
(before Eunice)

105

notes in day planner

I use a small day planner that fits in my purse, but there isn't always enough room for all the information I need to put in it. I write driving directions to new locations on a Post-it® Note and stick it right into my book so I always know where it is. Plus I keep a stash of notes in the front of the day planner and use them to expand its limited writing space.

Laya S., Abilene, TX

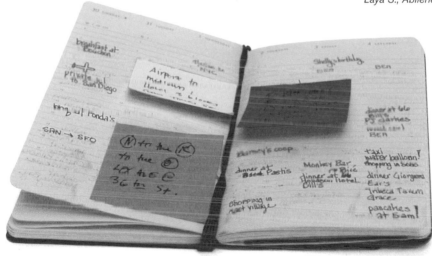

106

grab-'n'-go shopping

I keep a pad of Post-it® Notes on my refrigerator so that I can scribble down grocery needs as they occur. Before I head to the store, I pull off the current note and stick it to my purse. I don't lose my grocery lists anymore! As I cruise the aisles, I pull out my list and stick it onto the cart's handle so I can see what I need. It sure takes the headache out of shopping for groceries.

Carol W., Los Angeles, CA

107

sticky "magnets"

I was used to sticking to-do notes and other important reminders on my refrigerator door with colorful magnets. Then we got a new fridge with a stainless-steel door, and the old magnets wouldn't work. Post-it® Notes are the perfect replacement, combining note-taking and sticking power in one handy item.

Sue J., Atlanta, GA

108

grocery coupon notes

I use Post-it® Notes on my grocery coupons. Those tiny expiration dates are hard to read when you're shopping. So I put the notes on my coupons and write the "use by" dates right on them. You can't believe what a help it is.

Judith T., Mt. Juliet, TN

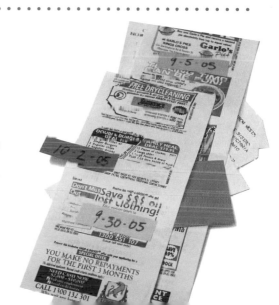

109

eye on the prize

I keep important goals in plain view by writing a brief reminder on a small Post-it® Note. That way, when my life gets hectic (as it always does), I am always able to see the big picture in spite of everything going on around me.

Kathleen P., Itasca, IL

110

meeting goals, step-by-step

As a professional organizer, I frequently use a system of Post-it® Notes to help my clients grasp the many steps required to accomplish a particular task. On the front of a file folder, I write a goal. Then the client and I will brainstorm all the steps required to achieve that goal. We write each step on a note and attach it to the inside of the file folder, which makes it easy to reorder tasks if necessary. When a task is completed, we remove the note, giving the client satisfaction that he or she is one step closer to the goal. Many chronically cluttered people have a difficult time picturing a process when they are completely surrounded by chaos. Using Post-it® Notes helps them clearly visualize what they need to do so they can achieve the success they seek.

Judith K., Plainville, CT

111

time management

Juggling tasks can be tricky for us all, so it helps to plan each week. I set aside some time, ideally on the weekend, to look at the week ahead. I make a list of tasks I have to do, prioritize the list by number, then write each numbered task on a Post-it® Note. I stick the notes into my day planner or calendar according to the date on which I need to complete them. As I finish each task, I either remove the note or move it to the next date on which I need to take care of that task again (as with paying monthly bills). Color-coding the tasks by project creates more effective visual reminders.

Ian M., Calgary, Canada

112

tips for to-do lists

For things I must do the next day, I write them on a large lined Post-it® Note and stick it on the pull-out shelf of my desk. Since the to-do items are for just one day, the note gets thrown out each night. If something didn't get done, then I transfer it to tomorrow's note. I never have more than the one note there, so it doesn't get cluttered and confusing.

Sheila M., Upland, CA

113

a reminder you can't miss

For some reason, if my reminder notes lie flat, I don't pay attention to them. So I turn Post-it® Notes into 3-D reminders. First, I write my to-do item on a note's adhesive side. Next, I tear the note slightly, just across the adhesive strip, and pull the two sides together. One side of the adhesive strip sticks on top of the other side. My note now stands up straight, and I use the remaining exposed sides of the sticky strip to place the note wherever I want. It's always easier to remember something when it's staring you in the face.

Lois T., Nashville, TN

Artwork by Georgina Dimitropoulos

114

planning far ahead

It's often necessary to schedule medical or dental appointments a year ahead—often beyond the range of a current paper calendar. When I make an appointment far in the future, I write it down on a Post-it® Note, along with the doctor's name and phone number, and stick it to the last page in my current calendar. When I purchase the next year's calendar, I move those notes to the date a week ahead of the appointment and write the appointment on the correct date. That bright note keeps me from forgetting critical appointments—and if I need to change anything, the phone number is right there.

Joe R., Nashville, TN

Artwork by Crystal Rae

115

a navigational necessity

I make frequent flights in my single-engine prop plane, and I rely greatly on maps that used to get marked up and damaged. I've discovered a great way to mark my maps quickly without damaging them. I use Post-it® Notes as arrows to chart my waypoints and to track mileage and fuel consumption as I fly. They're easy to see and let me use the same maps again and again.

John O., Belvedere, CA

keep it
together

"That's all you need in life—a little place for your stuff," observed comedian George Carlin. Nowadays, many people feel like their lives are filled with way too much stuff. It's no surprise that organizing is a hot topic, with stores, magazines, and TV shows devoted to the subject, providing lots of advice. As you tackle your clutter, simply remember there needs to be a place for everything—and everything in its place.

making order out of chaos

Been bitten by the spring-cleaning bug? Feeling the urge to purge? Conquer clutter one drawer or shelf at a time, tossing those items whose time has come. Then sort out what's left. Who knows? You may rediscover a forgotten favorite.

117

navigate the junk drawer

I sort my junk-drawer items by size or purpose into sealable plastic bags. If the contents are not easily identifiable, I create a label for them with a Post-it® Note, then stick it to the inside of the bag, adhesive side facing out.

Marieke B., Rotterdam, Netherlands

116

bake-sale ingredients

So many people have food allergies that I like to list the ingredients of anything I make for a bake sale for church or my kids' school. After securely enclosing the food and the plate in clear plastic wrap, I clearly write all of the ingredients on a Post-it® Note and stick it to the bottom of the plate for easy reference.

Alma P., Carthage, MO

118

prioing to sell

When preparing for a garage sale,
I color-code items with Post-it® Notes to
make pricing easier. Each color signifies
a different price. Then I make a simple
wall chart for customers that shows how
the note colors correspond to the prices.

Lorelei L., Knoxville, TN

75¢

$5

$2

119

tracking holiday gifts

To get a jump on the holidays, I buy gifts throughout the year. After wrapping them, I stick a Post-it® Note on each gift listing both the contents and the intended recipient. When the time comes, the notes ensure that I match the right gift tags to each package. For packages that I need to mail, I leave the notes on until I get to the post office to be sure that the mailing cartons are packed and addressed correctly.

Leslie H., Jersey City, NJ

120

sorting christmas lights

After we have taken down and bundled our holiday lights each January, we wrap Post-it® Notes around the bundles of lights to identify which ones fit where in our home—for example, on the stair railing or around the living room window.

Julie H., Oakland, CA

121

de-clutter day

Can't get through the mounds of clutter in your house? Use Post-it® Notes to simplify your life. First choose a day and write that date down on a note. Stick it where you can't miss it, to help keep you focused on your goal and allow time to organize. If it seems hard to de-clutter everywhere, then choose one room, one shelf—even just one drawer. On De-clutter Day, get five large cardboard boxes and a pad of notes. Write "Toss" on one note and stick it on a box. Stick "Fix," "Give away," "Keep," and "Sell" notes on the other boxes. Choose your target spot and remove one item at a time, putting it into one of the boxes. Then return only those items in the "Keep" box, taking the appropriate action with the contents of the other boxes. For example, load the "Give away" and "Toss" boxes into your car and head first to the consignment store, then to the recycling center. Finally, reward yourself. You've earned it.

Regina M., Boston, MA

122

turning what to wear into an organized affair

I used to dread going to my closet every morning, trying to decide what to wear. A friend came over to help me sort through all my clothes. I tried everything on until we decided which outfits made me look and feel good—and which ones were ready to be retired! We made a list of key pieces and then found every possible combination each could go with. We then listed each outfit, with accessories, on a Post-it® Note—and stuck all those on a larger sheet with the key item listed at the top. My lists are lined up on the inside of my closet door. Now my mornings are a breeze! I even add a tiny note if an item is at the cleaners or needs repair.

Fiona T., London, England

Artwork by Charlene Lau

123

dust bunnies, step aside

I use the space under my beds to store extra linens, seasonal clothing, and other items in clear plastic containers. I list the contents of each container on a large Post-it® Note, adhesive side up, stuck to the inside of the lid. I keep a duplicate note inside my utility closet so I can keep track of what's stored where without having to bend down to check.

Jane L., Columbus, OH

124

showtime anytime

Since my husband works the late shift, we can't watch our favorite television shows or sports events together. So I tape these programs every week. As I set up my VCR to record each night, I write down the name of the show on a Post-it® Note and and then stick it to the VCR. When the tape pops out, I stick the note on it. This way, I always know what's on each videotape.

Christine C., Joliet, IL

125

cropping photos

When I'm ready to frame my photos, I sometimes want the final image to be a different shape or size than the original. Rather than marking up the prints with a pen, I use Post-it® Notes to frame the images just the way I like them.

Deanna J., New York, NY

126

easy photo organization

When I order photos from the lab, I get doubles so that I can give copies to family and friends without delay. I sort them and put them into an album or in the mail shortly after they arrive at my house, and I always use Post-it® Notes to help sort them. I write the name of the person to whom I want to send each duplicate on a note and stick it on the photo, knowing that it won't harm the photograph. I also use Post-it® Notes as file tabs when organizing my own photos into storage boxes; they stick on easily, and there's no messing with hard-to-insert tabs.

Joanna R., Houston, TX

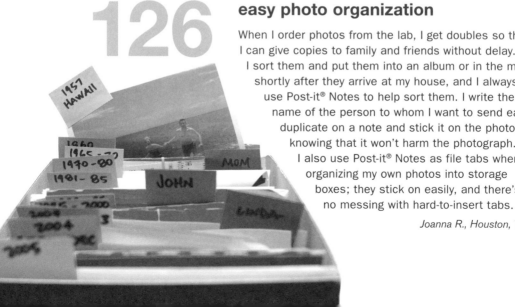

127

mending memo

As I toss clothing into my laundry
hamper, I stick Post-it® Notes on any
holes, rips, tears, broken zippers,
or missing buttons that I've noticed.
I also flag stains that need prewashing
treatment as soon as possible after they
occur, since I might forget later.

Sinead K., Dublin, Ireland

Artwork by Adam Marien

the morning rush—resolved

Want to start your day on top of the morning chaos of eating, dressing, and dashing? In the evening, gather your thoughts and pull together what you'll need for tomorrow. You'll walk out the door in style and in control.

128

last chance before you go

I put Post-it® Note reminders on the inside of my front door—for myself or the kids—to return library books, to pick up a teammate for soccer practice, to move my car for the street cleaners, or anything that we're likely to forget in the rush out the door.

Julie H., Oakland, CA

129

mirror reminders

I rely on Post-it® Notes to help me remember early-morning appointments. I put a note on the bathroom mirror to remind me of any way in which I'll need to deviate from my normal daily routine.

Marcella B., Los Gatos, CA

130

managing a wardrobe

I stick Post-it® Notes on the hangers for my jackets and suits, noting when I last wore each item and for which occasion. That way, I never come to a meeting or event in the same outfit twice in a row.

Morgan T., Raleigh, NC

131

waking up for work

My favorite way to use Post-it® Notes is as a gentle wake-up reminder. I have a habit of hitting the snooze button again and again. Because I do shift work and my schedule changes so much, in the haze of sleepiness I often can't remember what time I actually have to get out of bed. So, before I go to sleep, I write on a note the absolute latest time I can sleep, and I stick it on the wall beside my bed. When the alarm goes off, I don't just check the clock before deciding whether to hit snooze—I also check the note!

Leigh C., Calgary, Canada

cook's helpers

Whether you're a cook who relies on inspiration or one who goes strictly by the (cook)book, make life easier for yourself by using Post-it® Notes. Jot down variations on an old favorite recipe or remind yourself to pick up essential pantry items to fuel your next feast.

133

braille cooking instructions

Although I use magnetic tape to make braille labels for canned goods, it's easy to stick brief braille cooking instructions on Post-it® Notes on convenience foods such as dinners in a box, macaroni and cheese, and baking mixes. Post-it® Notes hold braille letters' raised dots long enough for repeated reading.

DeAnna Q., Colorado Springs, CO

132

baking reminder

The timer on my stove is broken. So when I put a dish in the oven and then head back into my home office to work, I write the time when the dish will be done on a Post-it® Note and stick it on my computer monitor's frame. No more burned meals!

Tina M., Merrill, WI

134

developing recipes

I have a website devoted to beer and food, with recipes I've created that use beer as an ingredient. As I develop the recipes, I use colored Post-it® Notes to track the steps in their preparation. I assign a different color to each key ingredient (such as pink for beef). I write down all of my preparation instructions step-by-step on individual notes. That way, I can keep track of changes and substitutions as I work on the recipe.

Lucy S., Milwaukee, WI

corral your filing system

Do you ever get the feeling that your filing system is out of control or, worse still, that it controls you? Make it your goal to handle each piece of paper only once by taking action on it, filing it immediately, or throwing it out.

135

organizing hanging files

Instead of creating file tabs right away for my hanging files, I organize them first using Post-it® Notes. I turn the pad with the adhesive edge facing me and write each category name on a separate note. I then stick it to the hanging file with the adhesive edge down and the name up. Once I'm satisfied that I have suitable names for all the categories, I replace the notes with printed file tabs.

Julie J., Gresham, OR

136

temporary binder tabs

When I want to organize a stack of papers into a three-ring binder, I use Post-it® Notes to create temporary tabs. I stick one on a blank page to start each new section, rearranging other papers and creating new divisions as I go.

Tina M., Merrill, WI

137 structuring files

I help clients create efficient filing systems, and I use Post-it® Notes in different colors to denote the umbrella categories, subcategories, and sub-subcategories, and even the names of the individual file folders. Because it's harder to move around the files themselves, we just move around the notes, and add or delete notes until we've fine-tuned the system. Of course, I include Post-it® Notes in the list of supplies my clients have to pick up before our first session.

June S., Los Angeles, CA

138

medical reimbursements

When I mail a copy of a medical receipt to my insurance company for reimbursement, I often have to remind it to pay me and not the doctor. I always write a message on a Post-it® Note, so that I don't have to write on the receipt itself.

Meryl E., Plano, TX

139

confidential copying

When photocopying papers that contain confidential information, I use yellow Post-it® Notes to cover up items that I don't want seen in the copies. They work like a charm, and no one can even tell.

Stacy H., Bloomington, IN

140

cleaning up copies

Before making copies of or scanning any documents that contain streaks, spots, or gutter shadows from previous copying, or that contain fax machine date and time lines, I use yellow Post-it® Notes to conceal those imperfections. I also use them to cover up information on the only version of a fill-in-the-blank form that I need to photocopy. Post-it® Notes save me tons of time and result in splendid, clean copies.

Leslie H., Jersey City, NJ

141

labels for file cabinets

Post-it® Super Sticky Notes make perfect labels for file cabinet drawers. Just fold (or cut) them in half, jot down the name, and slip them into the metal bracket.

Lynne J, Chicago, IL

142

personal banking

I use Post-it® Notes to jot down my bank account information on checks when a friend makes deposits for me. I've also used them to record my account information directly on a check when I've run out of deposit slips or when the ATM is out of envelopes.

Leslie H., Jersey City, NJ

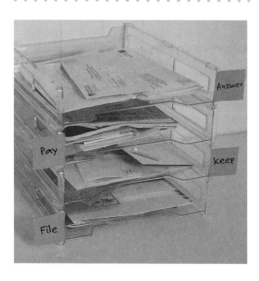

143

sorting paper piles

I used to get buried under a pile of papers, until I figured out a way to dig myself out. I put four filing trays in the room where I open my mail, then labeled each one with a Post-it® Note marked "Pay," "Answer," "File," or "Keep." Any paper that comes into my house goes into one of the trays as soon as I open it. As I pay a bill, I stick on a small note with the amount, payment date, and check number (or receipt number if paying online or by phone), then I move paid bills to the "File" tray. I also try to reply immediately to the papers in the "Answer" tray. Once I've taken appropriate action, I attach a small note with the day's date and place the item in the "File" tray. The "Keep" file is for items that I want to keep but that are not suitable for filing. I make a weekly decision on what to do with them. This simple system saves me from drowning in a sea of paper!

Anne R., Spokane, WA

144 off-the-wall (or -window) sorting

As a professional organizer, I use Post-it® Notes as markers
for sorting papers. If a client has huge piles of papers
that need to be sorted, I write the major categories of the
client's filing system on notes and then place them around
the room on the walls or windows above the sorting areas.
Once everything has been sorted and filed away, the notes
come down—and order is restored.

Ellen L., Seattle, WA

lights, camera, action!

Putting on a show requires coordinating many creative efforts, from scriptwriting to lighting, sewing costumes to acting. Keeping lines of communication clear among all participants helps guarantee the show is ready when the curtain rises!

145

designing theatrical lights

I work as a lighting designer for a theater company. As we progress through the weeks of rehearsals, we discuss how the scenery, lighting, and sound will affect the story. We use a tremendous number of Post-it® Notes on the script, knowing that the notes will change during each rehearsal. I watch and place a note on the page anytime I would like the lighting to change onstage. I use different colors for different types of cues or sets of operators. Before I started using Post-it® Notes, my scripts contained illegible collections of scribbled numbers and notes written in the margins, all connected with long arrows. Now, I am able to add, subtract, or move any of my cues with great ease. And color-coding allows me to keep track of which operator is taking which cue in which order.

Steve M., Oakland, CA

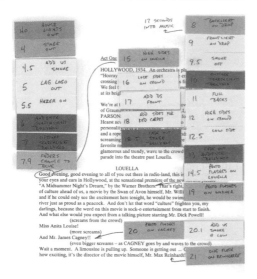

146

stage left!

As a theatrical stage manager, I use Post-it® Notes to mark in my prompt book all of the cues that I have to call during the show. Each kind of cue gets a different-colored note. My lighting cues, for example, are always in blue.

Lauren L., Crownsville, MD

147

making the (script) cut

I work for the TV soap opera *The Bold and the Beautiful*. We could not survive without Post-it® Notes. We use small ones as markers in the scripts, sticking them out the sides. This way, the supervising producer knows what pages to look at and can immediately decide what stays and what hits the floor of the cutting room.

Diana M., Burbank, CA

motivating

"The really great," said Mark Twain, "make you feel that you, too, can become great." Be really great and keep an eye out for ways to pass along positive vibes to the people around you. Small gestures—a brief word, a note of love or encouragement—add up over time to make a big impact. Your positive energy will stir the people around you to do better work—or simply to have a nicer day.

get juiced up!

We've all known people who just seem to have a great attitude—who work smarter and play harder. We could all benefit from inspiration and motivation in our lives. One secret to doing so is to find ways to keep your eye on the big picture—and stay positive along the way.

148

everyday inspiration

I write inspirational quotes on Post-it® Notes and stick them in places around my home, like on my computer or the bathroom mirror. I leave them up only for a short while, but it's cool to get a little inspiration everywhere you look when you're feeling down!

Diane M., Burbank, CA

149

mental health break

My work involves helping overextended midlifers balance their focus on job performance with frequent pauses for renewal. Visual reminders help. I encourage folks to put key words on Post-it® Notes to help them feel calm during the day: "Breathe," "Pause," "Laugh," and "Think!" All are great thoughts with positive results when encountered during a busy day.

Patricia K., Saskatoon, Canada

150

stopping a foul habit

While attempting to quit a long-term smoking habit, I was looking for any kind of help I could find. Because I've always been a big fan of Post it® Notes, it occurred to me that using them for positive (or negative, depending on which way you look at it) reinforcement would be a great help. I sat down with a pad of notes and a pen, and wrote one reason to quit on each note: "lung cancer," "face wrinkles," "stinky smell," "burn marks in clothes," "wasted money," "emphysema," "stained teeth," "asthma," and so on. Then I stuck the notes at eye level throughout the house. Everywhere I looked there was a reason to quit. I was off cigarettes within two weeks and have never gone back to them —16 years now! It was kind of funny—a longtime friend who was a heavy smoker happened to drop by for a visit while I had all my notes up. They stressed him out so much, he went home early!

Pat G., Colfax, CA

151

workout reminder

I'm a lifestyle and fitness expert, and I'm constantly recommending that my clients use Post-it® Notes as reminders to work out, drink water, eat in moderation, and so on. I tell them to place the notes on their desks at work, in their car, or on the TV screen. One client puts a Post-it® Note that says, "Just eat one serving of eight almonds—not the whole bag!" on his favorite snack. These visual reminders can constantly encourage people to live a healthy lifestyle.

Cyndi T., Woodland Hills, CA

Off the couch!

152

how about those sales reports?

mini pep talks

The sales department in our office has a goofy frog statue. We love to write comments on Post-it® Notes and stick them onto the creature as if it's saying things such as "Get going on your calls!" The statue gets secretly deposited on someone's desk if he or she needs a little good-natured prodding. My employees started it—and I occasionally get it on my desk, too!

Andrea G., Tucson, AZ

153

indirect communication

Years ago, I used Post-it® Notes in an exercise. I'd take a small note and stick it on the front of my shirt during an interactive presentation, and time how long it would take for someone to mention the note or ask what it was doing there. Often we'd get through the entire presentation without anyone mentioning that Post-it® Note, even though they'd all wonder about it and talk about it during the breaks. The point of the exercise was this: Just because people don't comment directly to you about something (poor service, a lousy attitude, or an unprofessional appearance), that doesn't mean they don't notice it.

Barry M., Helendale, CA

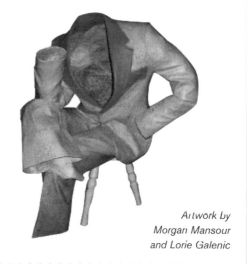

*Artwork by
Morgan Mansour
and Lorie Galenic*

154

under-the-seat surprise

As a speaker, I occasionally put Post-it® Notes under certain attendees' seats. It's the perfect way to indicate prizes they have won, tasks they will be asked to perform, or teams they will be assigned to. The notes are ideal because they're never noticed until I point them out. So attendees don't alter or move them, and the surprise is revealed only when I want it to be.

Barry M., Helendale, CA

spread the love

One of the best ways to brighten the day for your family is to cache away little notes. Those unexpected surprises that appear in lunches, purses, briefcases, computers, or calendars are the perfect way to share advice, encouragement, and humor with those you love.

155

love notes to a teen

I use Post-it® Notes to leave messages of love and encouragement for my teenage daughter because right now she's way too cool to acknowledge me.

Dan H., Lake in the Hills, IL

156

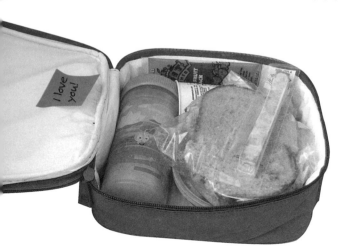

lunch box love

I often use Post-it® Notes to leave secret love notes in my kids' book bags or lunch boxes. Every now and then during their day, they find a little surprise message from Mom.

Peggy U., Chesterfield, MO

157 reward chart for good behavior

When we were teaching our preschooler to get dressed, comb his hair, and brush his teeth (without the constant reminders), we created a reward chart using Post-it® Notes. We let him know what our expectations were and explained that each time he did what was required without prompting, he'd get to stick a note on the chart. When he completed his tasks for a whole day (and later for a week), we rewarded him with an extra story at bedtime, a ride on the zoo train, or a new box of crayons. He loved tracking his own progress!

Jessica L., Alameda, CA

158

launch a romance

If you've never let fly an airborne love note, this sleek jet is the perfect delivery mechanism. My husband and I met each other at work. We'd use Post-it® Notes folded into gliders to exchange romantic airmails detailing our next rendezvous.

Emma F., London, England

LET'S GO TONIGHT!

Artwork by Stefanie Korab

159

love notes to spouse

I use Post-it® Notes to write love notes and messages to my husband. I tuck them into his briefcase, stick them on the rearview mirror, or attach them to anything he's likely to encounter during his day. These small surprises let him know that I'm thinking about him!

Tina M., Merrill, WI

Artwork by Alex Leitch

secret-agent dog

I have a corgi named Nikki. When I want to send my husband a message while I'm in another room of the house, instead of yelling, I stick a Post-it® Note message on Nikki's collar. He knows what to do and runs right to my husband. What is a game for Nikki makes life that much easier for us!

Joanne S., Albuquerque, NM

cream and sugar?

When I work at home and need a cup of tea, I call in my dog. I pop a Post-it® Note on her collar with the scribbled message, "Make me a cuppa!" Then I tell her to find my husband, who in turn makes me some tea. This system has about a 95 percent success rate.

Heather M., Sydney, Australia

162

love notes

To surprise my boyfriend in a wonderful way, I did something I knew he'd really love. I took an entire packet of small Post-it® Notes and wrote "I love you" on every note. I covered his room with them. I hid them in places he'd find later on, as well as stuck them in obvious places, such as all over the walls and the ceiling. He was so surprised when he came home that night, and to this day he's still finding them. But the sweetest thing was, one day when I came home I found *my* entire room covered in Post-it® Notes that said, "I love you more."

Selena P., New Orleans, LA

163

bikes beware!

My wife likes her bicycle almost as much as she likes me (or vice versa). Unfortunately, she often forgets when it's on top of her car—three bikes have now lost the battle with low-clearance garages. I started sticking a Post-it® Note with "Bike!" on it on the inside of the windshield to remind her that her bike is on the rack (and that she's in my thoughts).

Derek W., Homewood, CA

Artwork by Kim Gorman

raising
a family

"Our greatest natural resource," noted dream-maker Walt Disney, "is the minds of our children." When faced with all the chaos of daily life, it's easy to feel sometimes as if you aren't always nurturing your kids as well as you could. Fortunately, handling the small, everyday details in imaginative ways can help the greatest natural resource in your life—your children—flourish.

taking care of (baby) business

Sleep-deprived new parents are guaranteed to forget things (when did he last eat?) and run around spinning their wheels. Help look after your baby's needs—and your own—by taking note of some of the details of daily life with baby.

164

keeping track of twins

I have twins and used Post-it® Notes to keep track of which baby bottle belonged to which baby and when I last fed them. The notes worked great and never left any sticky residue on the bottles.

Sandra L., San Francisco, CA

165

changing-table display

When my daughter was an infant, I drew simple pictures on square Post-it® Notes and stuck them on the wall beside her diaper-changing table—well out of her reach. Looking at the pictures kept her occupied and happy while I was changing her.

Cindy E., Oakridges, Canada

166

shhh, baby's sleeping

After our daughter was born, my father-in-law came to help out for several weeks. He relished his role as a new grandfather, and he performed it with great diligence, leaving reminders everywhere on Post-it® Notes. My wife even found one on the seat of her car saying, "Close door quietly when the baby's asleep!"

Chris H., Fremont, CA

167

making friends

My brother and his wife came to visit with their two children, one a bashful 18-month-old girl. Try as we might, she just wouldn't warm up to us but instead kept walking back and forth, ignoring us. As I was watching her, I saw a pad of Post-it® Notes on the coffee table and the thought occurred to me that they just might get her attention. So every time she walked by me, I stuck a note on her clothing. After I'd used the whole pad, she was smiling, and we became fast friends. I've since used the same trick with several other small children, getting similar results every time!

Karl N., Broken Arrow, OK

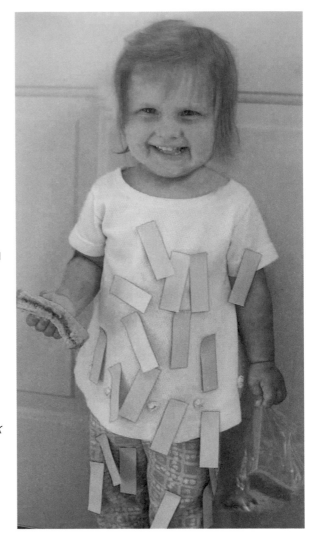

168

amusing the kids

This sounds nuts, but when my kids were little, they absolutely loved it when I stuck Post-it® Notes on them. As they figured out how their hands worked, they loved pulling off the notes. I would give the older kids a whole pad of notes to pull apart and stick on things, or to draw on. Today, my computer monitor is decorated with the art gallery my five-year-old created while I was busy finishing up important work.

Stacey L., Oakland, CA

169

labor according to plan

When it came to writing down my birth plan, I was completely overwhelmed by the idea of actually giving birth. Finally, I thought that if I could fit my birth plan on a Post-it® Note, then I could probably handle labor. I wrote down just the things that were important to me (no drugs, for example) and stuck it right on the wall next to the bed where the doctor and labor nurse couldn't miss it.

Cindy B., Chicago, IL

keeping a family on the ball

In well-functioning households, all family members know what's expected of them—and all of them do it! Informal but organized schedules, chore charts, and calendars keep everyone in the know and working together.

171

teenage to-do lists

When my daughters were teenagers, I would leave Post-it® Notes on the doors to their bedrooms with tasks, reminders, or phone messages written on them. Once they had taken care of whatever they needed to do, they would throw away the notes, and I knew that the tasks were done. I still do this when they are home, though they're 24 and 28 years old. The system still works.

Sherry R., Berkeley, CA

170

put a lid on it

I put Post-it® Notes on household items to remind my kids to do their chores. For instance, I might put a note on the TV that says, "Dust me before you turn me on!" Or I'll put one on the lid of the toilet (the first place the kids head when they wake up) to remind them of something they need to do before school.

Tina M., Merrill, WI

10-minute–chore chart

I have a chart listing all of the jobs that need to be done around the house. I break them down into tasks that take 10 minutes or less to complete. Then I write each task on a Post-it® Note, color-coded according to difficulty, so that each kid can do an age-appropriate task. On Saturday morning, I start passing out the chore notes. The kids stick them on their sleeves to keep them focused. When they've completed a chore, they return the note to the chart for next week.

Ian T., Melbourne, Australia

Run a load of laundry

Pick up toys

Clean bathtub

Sweep front porch

Artwork by Jennifer Zilinski

173

pet-sitter prompts

Before we go on vacation, we use colored Post-it® Notes to make all the to-do lists as easy as possible for our pet-sitters. In addition to leaving a sheet of instructions, we write individual notes that provide easy-to-spot cues for everything they might need to keep our dog happy. One note identifies the closet where they'll find the leash—"Leash in here" —and another the hook it's hanging on. The same goes for the door to the cupboard where we stow the pet food.

Margaret A., Manchester, England

174

kitty curative

My sweet old cat has several prescriptions from the vet that keep her in tip-top shape. Since it's enough of an effort to keep track of my own medications, I write down which medicine I need to give her, how much, and when on a Post-it® Note and stick it on the door of the closet where I keep the cat food. That way I never forget, and she stays healthy, happy, and frisky.

Annie L., Savannah, GA

clever critters on parade

Children delight in folding paper into animals and other shapes. Use several different colors of the three-inch-square Post-it® Notes and turn your kids into origami experts! They'll be proud of the results—while also learning patience and precision.

175

easy origami

I'm a busy mom, but teaching our kids origami is simple with Post-it® Notes. The three-inch note size is just right, and the sticky edge lets us all be more creative with less effort.

Helen V., Pittsburgh, PA

To make your own turtle from a Post-it® Note, follow these steps:

1 Fold a note in half diagonally with its sticky strip on the inside.

2 Fold the top right and bottom left points inward, so you end up with a small square.

3 Crease the square along the diagonal, from the lower left to the upper right.

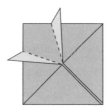

4 Fold the upper left corner's flaps as shown above, creating two of the turtle's feet.

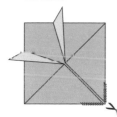

5 On the lower right corner, cut or tear the flap's edges a little so you can fold feet there.

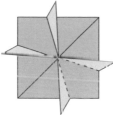

6 Fold the lower right corner's flaps as shown above, creating the second pair of feet.

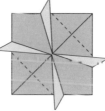

7 Fold in the upper right and lower left corners to form the turtle's body.

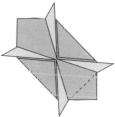

8 Fold down the lower right corner to make the first crease of the turtle's neck.

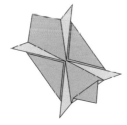

9 Finish the neck and form the head by folding the lower right tip out as shown.

10 Turn over and mark the eyes with a pen or pencil. Your turtle is now complete!

176

emergency gift wrap

I had to wrap a last-minute gift for my young daughter and discovered we were out of wrapping paper. Desperate, I covered the entire box in yellow Post-it® Notes, then simulated a ribbon and bow in hot-pink notes. She loved it!

Ellie T., Boise, ID

177

birthday treasure trail

On the eve of my kids' birthdays, we draw arrows on Post-it® Notes and use them to mark a path downstairs and through the house to where we have hidden their presents. We also add messages along the route saying things like "Happy birthday," "We love you," "Go this way," and "You're 9 today!"

Julie H., Oakland, CA

178

show me the love

I keep a running list of gift ideas for my wife on a Post-it® Note stuck in my wallet, so I'm ready for every birthday, wedding, anniversary, Mother's Day, and Christmas—or just for one of those "I love you, so here's a surprise" days.

Paul K., Portland, OR

Artwork by Chelsea Treahy-Geofreda

179

kids' height chart

When my son had friends over for his fifth birthday party, I made a height chart using Post-it® Notes. I stuck the notes on a wall in the shape of a palm tree (a ladder or a castle works well, too). Then each child stepped up to have his or her name recorded on the chart. They loved seeing and comparing their heights. An especially big hit was having a gift for the smallest child—since he's always on the short end of the stick.

Michelle B., Memphis, TN

180

note from the tooth fairy

When my kid loses a tooth, I compose a message from the tooth fairy on a small Post-it® Note and then fold it up to hold the all-important quarter under the pillow.

Dan A., Corte Madera, CA

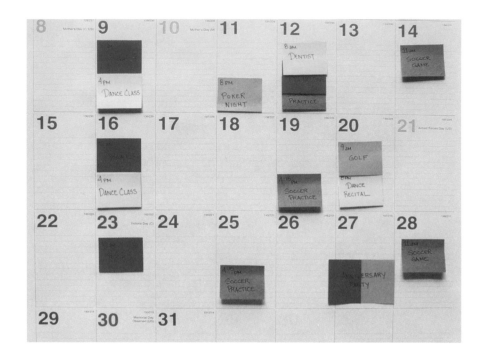

181 family organizer

Most families have multiple activities scheduled every week. A visible, color-coded family organizer is an enormous help for mine. I mounted a large wall calendar in the kitchen and assigned a different color of Post-it® Note for each family member to write his or her activities and commitments on. The notes are placed on the appropriate day, and even when we're all busy, it's easy to see who's doing what. Notes can be removed each morning and stuck in a lunch box, day planner, or briefcase as reminders.

Martha M., Davenport, IA

Artwork by Melissa Knight

travel

"The world is a book," marveled Saint Augustine, "and those who do not travel read only a page." Travel does indeed broaden the mind. Whether you're driving out of town for a weekend escape, hopping on a plane for a business trip, or setting out on a grand vacation tour, the more organized you are before you leave, the more pleasurable each new page of your journey will be.

traveling stress-free

Planning a vacation calls for a higher level of organization than most of us practice in our daily lives. For the stress-free break that you crave, find little ways to help you keep track of details when you are away from home.

182

mini travel dictionary

When traveling abroad in a country where I don't speak the language, I leave my dictionary in the hotel. Instead, I make up specialized cue cards on Post-it® Notes with basic words and phrases, then I stick them right in my wallet to make dining, shopping, or just getting around much simpler.

John R., Austin, TX

Key phrases
in Danish

tak — thank you
vær så venlig — please
velbekomme — you're welcome
hvor meget koster det? —
    how much does that cost?
snakker du engelsk? —
    do you speak English?

bøf = beef
kylling ("kiuling") = chicken
fisk = fish
røsted = roasted
bagt ("bakt") = baked
rød/hvid vin = red/white wine
øl ("pull") = beer
ost ("most") = cheese

183

currency conversions

I write out the currency conversions for whatever country I'm in on a Post-it® Note and stick it in my wallet. That way, I'm more confident when I am buying things, since I have a reminder of how much my bills and coins are worth.

Sven S., Malmö, Sweden

fun fact

A traveler found himself pulling an all-nighter at an airport. He wrote his flight information on a Post-it® Note, along with a plea to wake him up in time, and stuck it on his shirt. It worked— twice! He dozed off after one traveler woke him. The second person made sure he was up.

184

teaching a language class

I am a full-time English instructor in Taiwan. At the end of class each week, I teach my students the names of 10 things around the classroom. For beginners, I might stick to simple vocabulary words, such as "desk" and "window." For intermediate and advanced learners, I might teach them more-specialized words like "electrical outlet" and "smudge" (such as one on a window). At the beginning of the next class period, I give each student 10 blank Post-it® Notes, dictate 10 words from the week before, and ask the students to write each word on a note. Then they have to go around the room and put the notes in the right places. The first one who finishes gets a prize.

Hall H., Hualien, Taiwan

Q:
What is the future tense of "to sail"?

A:
vil sejle

185

foreign language quiz

I use Post-it® Notes for studying a foreign language. I write the questions on notes of one color, then each of the answers on notes of another color. Then I scatter the notes around the room and try to match them up again.

Peggy U., Chesterfield, MO

186

efficient packing lists

For years, I always forgot to pack one or two items when I traveled, and so wasted money and time buying new ones en route. Then I started making packing lists on Post-it® Notes. A few days ahead, I stick them to the dresser or medicine cabinet. As I think of new items, I add them to the lists, which I can then easily check off when packing.

Gretchen K., Helena, MT

187

duplicate itineraries

I make two copies of my itinerary, including addresses of hotels, on Post-it® Notes. I stick one inside the lid of my suitcase, the other inside the cover of my notebook. If my suitcase ever gets lost, whoever finds it also finds my itinerary—and, I hope, reunites me with my luggage at my next stop!

Peter C., Chicago, IL

188 mapping out city travel destinations

I like to get my bearings the moment I arrive in a new city, and I always travel with a pack of Post-it® Notes to help me out. When I check in, I ask for a map, then flag the location of the hotel. Before I begin each jaunt, I add flags of different colors for the places I plan to visit: yellow for museums and historical sites, blue for shops, green for parks and botanical gardens, red for restaurants, and so on. It sure beats lugging around a heavy guidebook or a file of website printouts.

Geoff C., Charlottesville, Va.

Artwork by Christine Vlasic

strange but true

A post-flight check in Minneapolis found a Post-it® Note affixed to the nose of a plane after a 1996 flight from Las Vegas. The note, intended for the plane's Las Vegas ground crew, survived take-off and landing after experiencing speeds of 500 miles per hour and temperatures of –56°F (–49°C)!

189

drawing for your supper

Back in my days as an art student traveling through Europe on the cheap, I used to keep a pad of Post-it® Notes in my backpack to sketch on with colored pencils in cafés and bistros. You'd be amazed at how many restaurant owners gave me a free glass of wine or even a meal in exchange for one of my sketches.

Regina P., Los Angeles, CA

Artwork by Paige Peressotti

190

explaining destinations

I am hopeless at pronouncing words in foreign languages and usually have taxi drivers scratching their head as the meter keeps running. Now I simply write my destination and the address on a Post-it® Note and hand it to the driver. I get where I'm going faster and save money at the same time.

Ron P., Gladwin, MI

Musée des
Beaux-Arts de Nice
33, Avenue des
Baumettes

191

personalizing travel books

I turn every guidebook into a travel journal with a pack of Post-it® Notes. As impressions occur to me when visiting a sight, I jot them down on a note and stick it to the relevant page in the book. At journey's end, I'm left with a highly personalized guidebook filled with fond memories.

Suzanne S., Illawarra, Australia

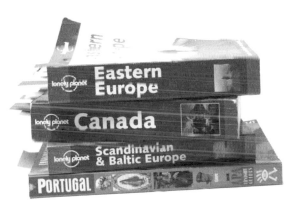

traveling with children

Every parent knows that it helps to keep children distracted during long flights or car rides. It's always a good idea to bring along fun games and familiar comforts from home to make their journey brighter—and yours easier.

192

portable board games

I make travel games to keep my kids amused while we're on the go. For tic-tac-toe, I make a grid by placing nine large square Post-it® Notes on a square piece of cardboard. Then I draw Os and Xs on two different colors of smaller notes. The children play the game over and over again. I keep all the notes stuck to the board for next time. For dominoes, I take a pack of small rectangular notes, draw a line down the middle of each, then place sticky dots to make the pieces: 42 notes with all the variations (1 + blank, 1 + 1, 1 + 2, and so on, through 6 + 6). The kids help with this. We keep the notes in a resealable plastic bag and stick the "dominoes" on the back of the tic-tac-toe board.

Debbie M., Sydney, Australia

193

time flies when you're having fun

When I had to travel by plane across the country with my two-year-old, I brought along pads of Post-it® Notes to occupy him during the long flight. To him, they were a novel toy with a wide range of possibilities: breaking off chunks of notes, attaching them back together again, sticking them all over everything, drawing on them, ripping and crumpling the papers, and so on. The miles went by as pleasantly as if he'd had an expensive new toy.

Caryn G., Berkeley, CA

194

window on the world

I keep a pack of the transparent, sticky Post-it® Flags in my pocket when we need to fly. My child puts them on the airplane window to create a stained-glass effect and is happy sticking and resticking them to his heart's content. It passes the time and keeps him from kicking the seat of the poor guy in front of us.

Miho A., Berkeley, CA

195

airborne artist

Medium-sized or large Post-it® Notes make great drawing pads on an airplane. Remove the backing sheet to stick a pad to either the seat tray or the window, transforming it into an easel. Before I had this brainstorm, I seemed to be spending half the flight reaching onto the floor or under the seat to get the drawing papers my child kept dropping.

Miho A., Berkeley, CA

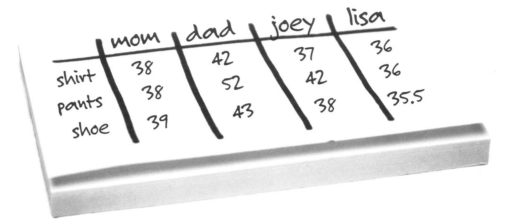

	mom	dad	joey	lisa
shirt	38	42	37	36
pants	38	52	42	36
shoe	39	43	38	35.5

196 clothing size translators

Before traveling abroad, I jot down the clothing and shoe sizes of my nearest and dearest on a Post-it® Note, with their sizes converted to those of the country I'm visiting. (These size conversions are easy to get from the Internet.) I stick the note inside the travel-documents wallet I carry with me. That way, with a quick glance, I can make sure any wearable gifts I buy will fit my friends and family.

Katie M., Washington, DC

197

clearing messages

When I travel, I need to remember to clear my home and business answering machines at least once a day. I write "Clear answering machine" on a bright neon Post-it® Note and attach it to the mirror in my hotel room. As a result, I never forget to clear my messages. When I'm not on the road, I keep the note in my bag of travel toiletries so I always have the note with me on a trip.

Barbara G., Killingworth, CT

198

credit card security

Whenever I travel, I write each credit card number and the card company's customer service number on two Post-it® Notes, hiding one in a secret place in my suitcase and one in my briefcase. If one of my credit cards is ever lost or stolen, I can quickly report it!

Art S., Des Moines, IA

working
it out

"I'm a great believer in luck," said Thomas Jefferson, "and I find that the harder I work, the more I have of it." Each of us is capable of making our own luck. Preparation, organization, and practice represent the foundation of good fortune. No matter what kinds of endeavors you want to undertake, finding ways to work smarter, not just harder, will help bring success within reach.

succeeding in the writing life

What's the difference between people who want to be writers and those who actually are? More often than not, it's all about staying organized. Keep track of ideas and projects to help those creative juices flow far more effortlessly.

199

writing a thesis

On my commute back and forth between school and home, I wrote my graduation thesis on Post-it® Notes. I even gave the final revision to my adviser in several blocks of notes in different shapes and colors. He told me he never knew anyone who depended so much on notes. When the time came to publish my thesis, he encouraged me to dedicate the work to 3M and Art Fry, the inventor of the Post-it® Note.

Socorro S., New York, NY

200

color-coding edits

When I'm editing a manuscript, I use different colors of Post-it® Notes to identify different types of editorial issues, such as author queries or inconsistent uses of a word or phrase. For example, I use one color to remind me to come back to a troublesome passage if I'm unable to resolve it right away.

Julie H., Oakland, CA

201

taking the mystery out of writing mysteries

This may sound weird, but my sister and I use Post it® Notes to kill people. Well, sort of. We're the coauthors of a mystery series featuring detective Louis Kincaid. Because our books are very clue-intensive with twisting plots, we sometimes find it hard to keep things straight. Kelly lives in Memphis and I live in Fort Lauderdale, so we've been trying to find ways to communicate back and forth. Post-it® Notes came to our rescue. We use yellow notes to keep track of our story line ("Louis finds the body" or "Killer confesses in woods") and stick them on a large board. It's very easy to move the notes around as we change the plot. We use bright blue notes to keep track of the "back story" (stuff we need to know that's going on but the reader doesn't). Pink and green notes denote "Change later" and "Check this fact." We're doing something right—our books have been nominated for all the big mystery awards and have gotten on the *New York Times* best-seller list! That's our story about Post-it® Notes, and we're stickin' to it!

P.J. P., Fort Lauderdale, FL

202

fine-tuning a novel

I use Post-it® Notes to finesse plot ideas, character development, and other details as I'm writing a book. Later, as I read through the notes, I jot down more ideas, each on its own note, then sort the notes onto larger sheets, by scene or chapter. This is how I improve my novels. I've used about 2,000 notes for my latest book!

Janet H., Reno, NV

*Artwork by
Alina Yanta*

Tip #18:
Catch up on correspondence while your child is asleep in the car.

203

writing a book tip by tip

I wrote my second nonfiction book entirely on Post-it® Notes. Because it's a book of 365 tips, I wrote each one on a separate note. I carried the pad of notes in my pocket and conveniently wrote a tip each time I thought of one.

Dawn C., Eugene, OR

204

portable planning

While writing my book a few years ago, I had to do a fair bit of traveling. The problem was, I needed to carry my notes with me, and my regular files were too cumbersome. Post-it® Notes came to my rescue. I bought several sizes and colors, each of which represented something different. Large yellow notes, for example, were chapter headings, while smaller yellow ones were paragraph titles, blue ones were content ideas, and pink ones were illustrations. I would put these notes on the wall facing my desk and sit back to think about structure and flow, easily changing the sequence and adding or eliminating items. When it was time to travel, I simply took the notes down, stuck them on top of each other in the correct sequence, put them in an envelope, and hit the road. At my hotel, I would stick them up again on a mirror or wall.

Jim C., Lake Sherwood, CA

205

reinforcing brand awareness

I use personalized Post-it® Notes to reinforce the branding of my two websites. I've had them printed with different slogans—some funny and casual, some serious and professional—and my URLs. Then I attach them to everything: notes to business acquaintances, thank-yous to reviewers, and articles I'm sending to friends. Each note is an easy way to remind people constantly of my brands.

Fern R., Newton, MA

206

mailing marketing brochures with ease

I have a local computer service business, and I regularly send out my brochure to other area companies. For each flyer, I cut off the colored end of a Post-it® Flag and then cut the sticky end in half. I use one half to attach a business card to the inside of the brochure. The other half holds the brochure closed for mailing. They work great, and the piece is easy to open without marring the card or brochure.

Mike P., Pawling, NY

207

promoting your band

I had preprinted pads of Post-it® Notes made for my boyfriend's band. I list the dates of upcoming gigs and pass them out at his shows so fans can stick them on their fridge or computer as reminders. They'll be great for getting the word out about their new album—if they ever finish it!

Liz L., San Francisco, CA

Phenomenauts

upcoming shows...
July 19 Slim's
July 28, 29 Bottom of the Hill

fine-tuning the perfect speech

A great speech lets you share ideas effectively, but very few things in life generate as much panic as delivering a speech to a large group of strangers. The key to success? Practice makes perfect—and Post-it® Notes can help.

209

numbering your thoughts

Start the speech-writing process by putting down every idea that comes to mind on a Post-it® Note. On an empty table or wall, begin sticking the notes in logical order. Rearrange them until all your points make sense and the transitions flow well. When you're satisfied with the sequence, number the notes in order, and use them to flesh out your speech.

Eve H., Chicago, IL

208

a margin of success

When I'm printing out a speech I've written, I set a very wide right margin. I use that margin to summarize the key points from the previous paragraphs on Post-it® Notes. When I give my speech, those bold notes serve as memory triggers and help me get back on track if I lose my place or forget my current idea.

Haydee G., Seattle, WA

210

in-your-face preparation

For business presentations, I fine-tune my delivery at home by summarizing key points on Post-it® Notes and arranging them in order around a mirror. Practicing aloud points out problems with flow. I rearrange the notes and repeat my delivery until the speech feels relaxed and I'm able to make my case powerfully. In the mirror, I check my facial expressions and gestures to make sure that they aren't distracting.

Andrew T., Orlando, FL

211

flexible outlines

As a speaker and an author, I constantly use Post-it® Notes to organize my writing, research, and presentations. I put one or two words reflecting what I want to say on each note, and I use them to create an outline of a speech. While speaking, I can compose on the spot by moving a note if needed. Post-it® Notes provide flexibility that regular paper just can't match.

Bob T., St. Louis, MO

212

handy reference tools

When I'm conducting a training session, I keep Post-it® Notes handy to flag a sheet on a Post-it® Easel Pad in case the group and I want to refer to that sheet later. This makes an old-fashioned flip-chart training session move faster and more smoothly than one delivered on a computer.

Ellen L., Seattle, WA

213

presentation to-do lists

In my roles of speaker and trainer, I often encourage attendees at my programs to write down random thoughts, concerns, or to-do items on a Post-it® Note as ideas pop into their heads. By the time the program ends, they've often already completed their to-do list or action plan!

Beth H., Menomonee Falls, WI

helping out at work

Workplace success is usually measured on a large scale: deadlines met, sales targets hit, strategic goals achieved. But don't forget that everyday small achievements can make your time at the office hum right along.

215

labeling lunches

Which lunch bag is mine in the office refrigerator? A Post-it® Note does the job. Now that I clearly label my lunch bag with my name on a note, it's rare that mine mysteriously disappears.

Leslie H., Jersey City, NJ

214

package pickup

In my office building, we leave packages out to be picked up by UPS shortly after hours in the unstaffed and unlocked lobby. I stick a large Post-it® Note on the front door to alert couriers that the lobby is open and that they can come inside to pick up the packages.

Leslie H., Jersey City, NJ

216

planning office layouts

Once when I shared a four-person office, we drew a layout of our space on graph paper, then cut out small pieces of Post-it® Notes (sized to scale, of course) to represent our desks, chairs, and other furniture. It took awhile to set up, but it was really easy to rearrange the "furniture." It was sort of the science-geek, low-tech method of interior design.

Janelle N., Berkeley, CA

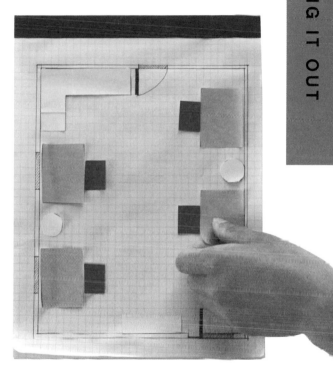

217

an unforgettable birthday

When my brother turned 40, we decorated his office with hundreds and hundreds of Post-it® Notes—each with "40" written on it. He couldn't believe it!

Gordon R., Sheffield, AL

218

training a new receptionist

When we train new employees to answer phones, we ask them to write the company greeting on a Post-it® Note and stick it on any phones they might answer. That way they learn the greeting quickly, feel confident, and don't stumble over their words. They keep the note stuck to their phones as long as needed, then remove it only when they have memorized the greeting.

Andrea G., Tucson, AZ

219

nailing the spiel

As a temporary employee, I move from job to job often. In each new assignment, I use Post-it® Notes to label any unmarked telephone lines I'll be answering with the full spiel for that particular line. I'm sure that's one of the reasons why so many companies like to have me come back to work again.

Leslie H., Jersey City, NJ

220

phone messages

I use Post-it® Notes to jot down phone messages. I keep a stack of small notes right next to my phone. When I'm making a call or checking my voice mail, I'll jot down notes to myself and stick these reminders on my very expensive note board — or, as I've heard other people call it, the "computer monitor."

Carol W., Los Angeles, CA

221

labeling phone extensions

Because we often swap desks depending on which team we're working with each month, we simply write everyone's names on small Post-it® Notes, or on cut-down large notes, and stick them on the phone buttons that dial our current numbers. That way we can easily reposition the notes as we change workstations.

Kevin J., Anchorage, AK

222

a visual plan of attack

I use Post-it® Notes for each separate aspect of project planning. I stick them either directly to the wall or onto sheets torn from large Post-It® Easel Pads. I decide which color Post-it® Notes will represent tasks that "Absolutely have to get done," and I continue down to "Nice to get done." When a task is complete, I place a check mark on it so I can see how I'm progressing. My office walls are covered with Post-it® Notes for every project I'm working on! I even roll up and store the notes and sheets after I finish projects for future reference in case I have a similar project to organize in the future.

Bette D., Pleasanton, CA

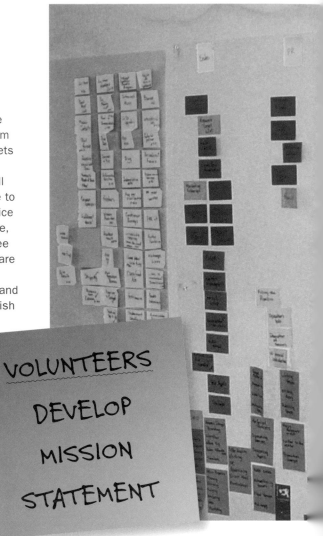

a final note

This book features more than 100,000 Post-it® Notes in its pages—and those are just the ones you can see. We used at least 7,000 notes to produce this book—to display ideas, mark changes, label photos, and keep track of our schedules and to-do lists.

NEED ARTWORK

managing time

IMAGE TK

index

Artwork by Matina Castonguay

Artwork by Tara Mulcahey

*Artwork by
Tamara-Rose Croxall*

The World's Largest Pink Ribbon, Times Square, New York City, October 2004